LAVUKISTAN

CITY OF BAUDINE

Out of the Loud Hound of Darkness

Also by
Karen Elizabeth Gordon

Karen Elizabeth Gordon

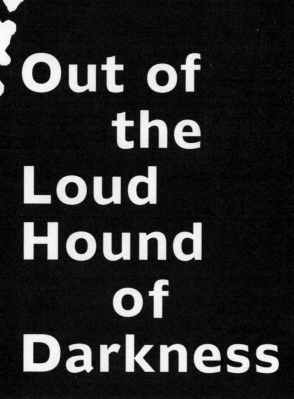

Out of the the Loud Hound of Darkness

a dictionarrative

pantheon books
new york

Library of Congress Cataloging-in-Publication Data

Gordon, Karen Elizabeth.
Out of the loud hound of darkness : a dictionarrative / Karen
Elizabeth Gordon.   p.   cm.
Includes index.   ISBN 0-375-40198-9
1. English language—Usage—Handbooks, manuals, etc.
I. Title.   PE1460.G59   1998
428—dc21   98-6739   CIP

Random House Web Address: http://www.randomhouse.com
Book design by Misha Beletsky
Printed in the United States of America
First Edition

9 8 7 6 5 4 3 2 1

In memory of
Thalia Polos
maker of shoes
mapper of hidden connections

Contents

Acknowledgments

Fervent thanks and unflagging affection for Luis Tomasello, Rastislav Mrazovac, Lisa Karplus, Alba Witkin, Holly Johnson, Catherine Maclay, Richard Press, Ann and Dikran Tashjian, Constance Hale, Lily Culver, Natasha Heifetz, Milo Radulovich, Camilla Collins, Paul Walker, Helen Watt, Shelley Wanger, and Maia Gregory. Without one house, which disappeared in this winter's storms, these pages could not have filled with their fictions, and I'm undyingly grateful to Grace Fretter for all the pleasures and books-in-progress her Cragmont house has set me free to explore.

Introduction

If you are only now tuning in to this Balkanalian tour of Babel, you may well wonder where you are. Our in-house cartographer, Jonquil Allegra Mapp, is out at the moment—on a secret mission to Trajikistan—and has left me with fragments of maps, scraps of history of these torn-off countries, with their vanquished tribes and comatose hordes, that have insinuated themselves into the folds and borderlands of mightier empires. It is up to Jonquil to figure out whether these countries engulf or enlighten one another, why their kings spend time in exile at each other's courts, and why Amplochacha is always the name of the capital city, no matter which land you're in.

Inexplicable, too, is why enclaves of speakers of exquisite English have sought refuge in this fractured, parallel world, allowing this alluring, horrific setting to continue a tale of our language through the eccentric authorities we first heard in *Torn Wings and Faux Pas*. Startling Glower and his colleagues here meet romance fiction authors Strophe Dulac and Nada Seria in the pages of *their* books, which are all the rage in Louvelandia, Azuriko, and Blegue.

Politics, war, and money keep up the centrifugal force of a world that mirrors our own, with its strife, its iniquities, its graceless lurching and ineluctable habit of dying. The Grim Reaper, in a battle of wits with a cunning baba, won't let us forget the last. Will she charm *him* to death?

This rambling rampage takes us through finesses of usage and untangles confusions of look-alike and not so synonymous words, now that the terrors of grammar have been confronted, taunted, and tamed in the two handbooks that came before: *The Deluxe Transitive Vampire* and *Torn Wings and Faux Pas*. The companion lexicon at the back explains words sporting daggers that appear in the first, longer section and adds an ample handful of its own, putting those words into action to continue the stories and keep the sandman and the Loud Hound of Darkness at bay.

The baby dragons are growing up, exploring the subterranean passages beneath the Schloss, while the nanny, au pair, panther, general factotum, and myriad guests carouse in its bedrooms and *grand salon*. Rousing themselves, as the dragon Pasha Partout cannot, they wander the gloomy corridors and the surrounding howling terrain, where Drasko Mustafović with his brigands and the elemental forces hold sway.

While language inhabits us much as those creatures haunt the Schloss, it is also a place in which we dwell, a surrounding we cannot leave. It came from the darkness, and so early manuscripts were *illuminated* to captivate the eye. In this manuscript, capricious monarchs and murderous geographical features darken these benighted kingdoms in trade and war, and treacheries threaten the fragile stability of Louvelandia, Azuriko, and Blegue. The wilder landscapes of Lavukistan, the Vaasts of Laponesia, and Trajikistan cast their shadows over the more settled, town-centered history of Eloria, Pakriatz, Alsmeer, and Baudine. And now these unruly motley characters join your shadow thrown across the page.

Dramatis
Personae

Alabastro a once and mournful king in his
muslin pajamas who's lost his beloved consort,
Dariushka

> **Amaranthia** a young and frisky widow, with a
> motorcycle called Caliban; general factotum at
> the Schloss

Natty Ampersand sex-changing language prima
donna whose male half succeeded at suicide
described in *Torn Wings and Faux Pas*; the
female half quit the racket to become Nada
Seria, writer of romance fiction, after a brief
spell as amanuensis to contralto Constanza
Zermattress

> **Trill Apasaguena** business mogul / entrepre-
> neur sans culottes: in fact, without any clothing
> but a tie—the man in the grey flannel suite

Troto Asfoblatz desperado with Byzantine
mutations and half the posse of the Pink
Antlers Saloon in search of him

> **Frodo Asgard** drama critic for the *Darkling
> Mirror,* rival rag of the *Passevitza Clarion*

Angie Canasta world-weary mother of Tanagra; has retired from the limelight to the moonlight, keeping a gigolo and apartment in Rome

> **Capriccio** escaped from a commedia dell'arte scenario to the court of Incognito VIII, who ruled Blegue and—ever so briefly—Azuriko, where Capriccio served the king through glory and infamy as his faithful, dog-eared retainer

Mog Cinders lepidopteric courtesan with chalet on Lake Sandali and cherubim caught in her diaphanous veils, sonnets clacking at her heels

> **Whiffle Clackengirth** composer of the opera *The Velveteen Rabble,* an aleatory nightmare of fifty acts with costume changes by the audience along with those of the tenors, altos, and sopranos

Cowboys at the Pink Antlers Saloon, within weeping distance of the Schloss; object of Yolanta's ongoing curiosity about lingerie among the Wild West cross-dressers, including Flip, Rip, Samson, and Zap

> **Dariushka** amateur alchemist and Alabastro's queen, who died of fright in her sleep

Gavril Dark politician of stormy persuasions and innocuous presence; son of partner at Dark and Rush, Solicitors

> **Dentist and robot** ubiquitous ballroom dance partners, heretofore inseparable

Frotteau Dessange and **Serafima Dos Equis** highly versatile and mercenary brigands and interlopers

> **Dragons: Alfina, Despina, Beau Romano, Saskiak,** and **Pasha Partout**—all still in their advancing childhood at the Schloss and evading the surveillance of half the staff

Strophe Dulac nom de plume of author of bodice-ripping metafiction: *The Duchess of Malfatti, The Emerald Settee, Creepy Suzette, The Bad-Tempered Cavalier, Tatiana's Bear*; contender for Tory Auslander chair at Amplochacha U.

> **Sigismund Lolotte Flint-Page** scholar besotted with early English, her greyhound puppy, and medieval history with all its trappings; last seen in Paris treading a vein of God up the haunches of Montagne Ste.-Geneviève

Cram Fossilblast iconoclastic stylist of prose
who's called himself the Whore of Babel; author
of both fiction and a multivolume send-up of
The Elements of Style; frequent visitor to a villa
in Louvelandia where this book took shape

> **Gallimaufs** on compliments terms with Nimbo
> Moostracht; friends of Count Ghastly, Miranda,
> and Jesperanda; son TROPO GALLIMAUF III went
> off to seek his fortune in his granny's velvet
> vault

Generals Ludović and **Pvbxtrz** addicts of
martial conflict and strategy, sleeping out with
the boys; perpetrating participants in
internecine war

> **Count Ghastly** the Wretch of Lugubria with his
> fitful reclusions and morbid parlor games

Startling Glower Restoration fop, playwright,
and mercurial, magnetic host of "Up Your
Eponym," popular television show on language
in all its permutations

> **The Grim Reaper** tussling with a baba, in whose
> parlor he's materialized; a close associate of
> the Loud Hound of Darkness and a delighted
> visitor at the Battle of Bluttenbad

Duchess Ilona a runaway experimenter in *modes de vie* seen hither and yon in many guises and some very strange company after deserting the duke with a mouthful of tarts; also in league with monarchists throughout these benighted lands

> **Incognito** a succession of kings including INCOGNITO I, who didn't like his officially suppressed given name; INCOGNITO V, a devotee of Flann O'Brien and thus a bicycle fetishist; and INCOGNITO VIII, noted for such scandals as the Cashmere Crisis and the case of the lapsed credenza

Jacaranda sidekick-on-the-prowl of Amaranthia and also niece of the rumpled, cherubic curator of the Immergau Museum who returned from a spa in Trajikistan a svelte shadow of his former self

> **Dante Kaputo** a ruffian in chintz, pursuing Dusty Saxon through the canyons of Azuriko and wherever else her flying skirts and lashing hair beckon him to follow

Katya winsome au pair at the Schloss who arrived innocent but soon caught on after a few evenings in the *grand salon*; a favorite companion of Drasko Mustafović, whom she visits at Hotel Artaud

>**Kristiana** her young and untamed cousin on the best of terms with this book's beasts

Loona ubiquitous celebrity since she first appeared as a cover girl standing on her toes in a windblown cape and a state of exalted expectancy; gave Laurinda a poltergeist as a wedding present

>**Loud Hound of Darkness** Is it a dog? Is it a wolf? Is that friendly fire or demonic sparks flying off its teeth? First appeared in *The Red Shoes and Other Tattered Tales*: "Down the alley slouched a beast en route to the apocalypse."

Jonquil Allegra Mapp geographer / cartographer apprenticed to the wisest man in Louvelandia since her brisk dismissal from Amplochacha U. for compulsive effrontery; met Duško Mustafović, or Drasko, Jr., on her first tentative trek through Trajikistan

Boris Marcelovsky coiffeur from Trajikistan who came to Blegue and set up in a chic salon with an operatic clientele

Maud queen of Blegue who studied English grammar with Zoë Platgut—a mind after her own heart; wielded her scepter with a few angora rabbits up her sleeve

Milanka faithful sweetheart of the unknowable soldier, whom she hardly ever sees or rumples on her bearskin rug

Miranda a passionate consumer of thrillers and romance fiction who refuses to succumb to sleep and lose late-night hours of reading; frequent visitor at Gallimaufs' and friend of Jesperanda; helped proofread *this* book, since her name indicates a capacity for seeing

Cedric Moltgang a critic at large and also at risk

Nimbo Moostracht Eurobanker with headquarters in Paris and branches throughout the kingdoms; uncle of Laurinda; summers in Azuriko with school chums and suspicious characters

Drasko Mustafović leader of brigands (the ones with fans and other diverting accoutrements) and absent owner of the Schloss, his family's demesne; keeps suite in Hotel Artaud for his private life and makes raids from his mountain fastness

Duško Mustafović as named by his mother; sometimes goes by name of Drasko Mustafović, Jr., since he's the brigand's illegitimate son; Jonquil's lover in Trajikistan

Placido a succession of monarchs who ruled Louvelandia as a peaceable kingdom through eras of decadence and strife

Zoë Platgut laconic, no-nonsense authority on grammar, usage, and style whose exotic childhood in an Arab emirate produced an unlikely upshot; once taught kindergarten and now spends vacations in Macedonian monasteries getting high on their liturgies

Joubert Plume posed as robber in Azuriko, according to a dossier; married to Nada Seria

Prolix prolific, proliferating kings of Blegue and, when hegemony has been in their hands, despots of neighboring states

Dusty Saxon nickname of the elusive obsession that keeps Dante Kaputo careering through the scenery on his frothing palomino

Gregor Schlaffenfuss a couturier who's dressed many a courtesan, prima donna, hausfrau, and celebrity; enlists the lyrical talents of Jesperanda Trost in the nomenclature of his creations

Sonia Tweazle Scronx nanny to the little dragons at the Schloss, and only resident there with a practical grasp of the Internet

Vargas Scronx her husband, also known as AELFRIC VALINTHROB (his medieval sobriquet), whom she once locked in a dungeon for the sake of his academic progress

Nada Seria nom de plume of the next incarnation of what's left of Natty Ampersand; author of *To Die in a Dirndl, Giovanna's Mortgage, The Temptation of Tristan le Fay,* and *Taxi to the Other Island*

Drat Siltlow percussive language pundit with fascinating parentage and hallucinogenic insights; raised by three maiden aunts in Appalachia until his voice cracked

Ziggie Spurthrast formidable, fearsome second mate of the *Scarlatina* with a gift for sabotage

Rafael Todos los Muertos journalist provocateur noted for the heated candor he elicits from his stellar interlocutors

Torquil cast-off beau of Jonquil Mapp, whose acquaintance he deeply made at the Last Judgment Pinball Machine Motel; was told to get lost at Amplochacha's cathedral beside the relics of Saint Archulaga

Laurinda Travers-Moostracht niece of Nimbo Moostracht who has reversed her maiden and married names; honeymooned in Lavukistan, Azuriko, and Trajikistan, where she divined a minotaur at Hotel Flambeau; once kidnapped by brigands with fans to Trajikistan: were they in cahoots with her husband? Uncle Nimbo was the target of demands for the ransom.

Jesperanda Trost writer in several genres and masquerades; contributor to literary review *Licking the Beast*

Troto the unknowable and unknowing epic soldier; no relation to the desperado

Dodeska Tutulescu vampire with several children and the very picture of devoted motherhood; see her portrait by novelist Rikki Ducornet in *Torn Wings and Faux Pas*

Yolanta bibliophile and multimediac expatriate rustling cowboys with her video camera and her intimating repartee

Constanza Zermattress a contralto from Amplochacha, with many liaisons in her viatic past, but only Mozart prevailed; writing her memoirs with help of Nada Seria; godmother of Laurinda Travers-Moostracht

Couplings and Confusions

Finesses of Usage

Cave Canem

Beware of the Beast Within

acidulous
assiduous

Acidulous contains acid and means slightly sour in taste or manner.

*A*n acidulous tone had crept into both sides of the conversation, her side with balsamic asseverations and cloying evasions, his with a bite of horseradish astride a malt vinegar redolent of London fogs, fish and chips, and tabloid treacle and gossip (it was, in fact, revolting).

To complement the fig, pistachio, and finocchio caprice, the chef whipped up an acidulous splash of hazelnut oil, oxalis, and lime juice, with a pinch of powdered pfeffernuss.

Assiduous means industrious, conscientious, diligent, constant in attention and application; unceasing, persistent.

*A*ssiduous and mindful of the most persnickety punctilio, Jacaranda filled in for the general factotum, Amaranthia, whenever she slipped off for a meeting of the Belladonna Mafiosi in the raffish capital of Blegue.

adapt
adept
adopt

Harboring the word *apt* in its midst, **adapt**
means to adjust, get used to, make suitable.
(The latter meaning you will find at work for
Jonquil under *amiable*.) **Adopt** means to accept,
take in, take as one's own. **Adept** is very skilled,
highly proficient, and, when used as a noun,
means one possessed of and blessed with such
capabilities.

*A*lthough the little vampire was adept at tying
and untying knots, she decided that this particular bondage (she'd been kidnapped by brigands
without a clue to her true identity—or species—
thanks to the cosmetic dentistry disguising the
acuity of her teeth) called for the combined arts
of seduction and use of her fangs, and so the
brigands, enticed into her orbit, one by one un-
derwent this sanguinary conversion, forsaking
booty for blood, jewels for jugulars, trinkets for
throbbing throats.

He's an adept at this sort of tomfoolery, all right.
With my own four eyes I've witnessed him up-
staging the prima donna of Amplochacha at a
gathering in her honor with his ambidextrous
sleights of hand, rabbits up his trousers, ventril-

6

oquisms through a laryngitic diva, and a rumble with a muzzled Doberman.

Jonquil adapted to the privations and rigors of Trajikistan's inns with grinning equanimity before discovering an auberge on the road to the Fissures of Fingblat, just past the three crags known as the Saturnine Yet Oversexed Sisters, whence no comely youth ever returns.

They adopted an attitude of Sturm und Drang as protective covering while they recovered their wits and sang-froid.[†]

Having bought a dilapidated château in the wilds of Louvelandia, Madame Tutulescu began visiting orphanages in Rumania and snapping up the most attractive little urchins through perfectly legal procedures of adoption for perfectly lethal purposes.

affinity

Well! Was I ever consternated when I pulled up a web page from "Up Your Eponym" (Startling Glower couldn't resist flaunting his ersatz erudition over yet another medium, especially since his producers started flashing his E-mail address at the end of the program—and he didn't even know how to use it!) on the true and limited meaning of **affinity**, and the prepositions it takes—so often has it been used for knack or aptitude in cahoots with *for*. What it really means is a feeling of kinship, an emotional bond, a sympathetic link, and the prepositions that follow it are *between, with,* or *to.*

*T*he affinity between Incognito VIII and Capriccio grew more consummate year by year—a telepathic rapport and total trust that enabled the pair of them to give the entire country the slip in the midst of that shoddy furniture affair.

"Do that beast and I ever have an affinity to each other!" wrote Laurinda of a chance encounter that swept her off her feet in the midst of her honeymoon. It wasn't the minotaur in the hotel pantry, either, but an imperial guard dog in charge of the little prince on whom she was paying a diplomatic call on behalf of her uncle Nimbo.

Her affinity with the panther enabled Kristiana to roam freely about and below the Schloss and explore at her leisure the passage that contained abandoned armaments and skeletons of prisoners from the vicious but efficacious skirmish with neighboring Azuriko.

9

almost
most

Zoë Platgut believes that the misuse of **most** instead of **almost** (for nearly) fits into a pervasive pattern: our passion for brevity, our haste to abbreviate, especially in speech; but those habits spill into our writing. "A curious paradox prevails here," writes Platgut, "for we are both kicked back and in a hurry."

*A*lmost everyone at the premiere glittered and sparkled,* and it was a great relief when the lights went down and the curtain rose on the first act of Clackengirth's opera.

Almost every day, nowadays, I pray for my country's deliverance from this band of smooth-talking thugs.

"Do you ever think our country's on a collision course of histrionic journalism?"

* In fact, following the sensible example of Mog Cinders—always a pacesetter in a crowd—those whose evening bags could accommodate such scruples whipped out their sunglasses and wound up escorting their blinded fellow spectators to seats less well situated than their tickets promised.

"Almost all the time."

Most has its place in instances such as these:

*O*dious is the most gentle, caring sadist who's ever asked permission to mistreat me.

"Count Ghastly is the most lugubrious wretch I have ever attempted to humor," wrote Golly Inchkeep Gallimauf in a memorandum to Jesperanda, who went on to write the depressing gothic bestseller *The Wretch of Lugubria.*

Most of the time, we leave the dog outside to frighten the knickers off muggers taking a break.

That's the most you're ever likely to see of the palace of Trajikistan's three kings.

alongside
alongside of

Zoë Platgut, in her fiercer moments, says **alongside** should never be followed by **of**. Even Drat Siltlow, who cites several lyrics* in which the preposition keeps the beat, concedes it's unnecessary.

Running alongside the lorry on the autobahn was a beast with a matted coat of black fur and sparks flying off its teeth.

A ship with Trajik flag, shattered bow, and tattered sails had pulled up alongside the *Scarlatina* in the Zardana marina before Ziggie Spurthrast set out on her morning sprint, her leopard skin cutoffs and tank top attracting the attention of a spotted cat in heat who'd recently escaped from the circus.

Alongside the River Oublique in the Valley of Mousserousque winds a footpath frequented by fauns with festering hoofs and runaways headed for the hinterlands who wish to purify their souls en route.

* from "Down in the Meanest Part of Town" and "Don't Hurt Me, Baby, I'm in Pleasure Mode Tonight"

although
though

Although and **though** are interchangeable as conjunctions, but one takes precedence over the other depending on which part of a clause or sentence you're in. To open a clause, *although* is the one on which to bestow your favor. In linking words or phrases, *though* is more often obliging, and in certain constructions only *though* is correct, as we'll see with both Manx Vulpino and the warrior/lover below.

*A*lthough we've never actually met, I feel I know you through and through—as if I had a hand or stake in your conception and every rite of passage since.

I sent him letters every day begging him to keep his distance—for his own safety as well as mine—although I secretly hoped, even expected, to find him hanging from my balustrade when I returned from my Serbo-Croat lessons with my consonants in distress.

Raving mad though I am about most of Manx Vulpino's work, I think that in his ballet *Torn*

Wings and Faux Pas he's gone too far—with sylphs squawking like a gaggle of goosed Valley Girls and ostriches of a certain age on point and attempting entrechats.

He was a fearless warrior though timid suitor whose knocking knees and bulging eyes habitually announced his arrival. Over an intimate dinner for three, four, or five (anticipating rejection, he usually invited several of his heartthrobs at once and thus wound up with a voracious harem on the tab), he would crush the crystal in his firm though terrified grip, fracture his anecdotes into evanescent glints, swallow his bow tie, and come back from the powder room to a fur coat in the cloakroom—and here his valor always returned when it came to defending the torpid wrap against its usual occupant attempting to reclaim it.

"Although my married name is Madame Joubert Plume, Nada Seria is my nom de plume," said the once-upon-a-time sex-shifter Natty Ampersand.

amend
emend

Amend means to set right, to change for the better, improve, and is brought about by alteration or addition, to a text, for example— resulting in an amendment. **Emend**, a more formal word, means to effect such changes in a scholarly or literary work, and here the upshot is an *emendation*.

$\mathcal{P}$rocedures to apply for the Tory Auslander chair at Amplochacha U. have undergone one brief amendment: henceforth, the bathing suit exhibition will be replaced by a competitive cookout while members of the jury play snooker and blindman's bluff in the buff.

On a lavish two-year fellowship from the Vast Monthrock Foundation, and with the help of research assistant Aldebrand Trottenkammer, Sigismund set out on an ambitious emendation of medieval scholarship: asserting that *Gossamer and the Green Light* was written by a courtesan and mother of three royal bastards destined for joint jestership as keepsakes of her liaison with the melancholic king.

If you don't emend your conclusions to this travesty of the traditions of cartography, young lady, you must renounce an advanced degree.

amiable
amicable
amenable

Amicable tilts more toward friendliness and peacefulness, as in amicable relationships, divorces. **Amiable** comes bearing the smiles of a sweet nature, a kind heart. The two words are quite close in meaning, but with different emphases. **Amenable** is less synonymous, and I shall summon back a robot and a dentist to explain. When the dentist declared himself not averse to a month in Buenos Aires,* he was amenable to the notion of such a trip—that is, tractable, open to suggestion, advice.

* A pronouncement he would live to regret: later in Brazil, during Carnival, the robot ran off with a Deux Chevaux mechanic and a bandoneonist from Bahia, and the dentist wandered Rio from one *batería* to another in search of his partner, whose costume-swapping metamorphoses further confounded the dentist's quest.

The rupture of relations between Torquil and Jonquil was far from amicable. Torquil stalked her on the boulevards, burned Eastern crosses on her balustrade, bombed her mailbox with incendiary marzipan, invaded her E-mail with insinuations and pseudonyms, and crashed her farewell party in an asbestos cat-suit sporting a battery-operated lashing tail with which he thrashed Jonquil before a roomful of incredulous guests.

Jonquil's own amiable disposition would not give way, however, and she'd sidle up to strangers in the street singing variations of "Don't Be Cruel" she'd adapted for her ex's ire.

anodyne
androgyne

An **anodyne** is a cure, a palliative, a source of soothing comfort; as an adjective, it means capable of bestowing comfort, eliminating pain; relaxing: anodyne brochures from the Azuriko tourist bureau promising melodious brooks and purling streams, beneficent mists from waterfalls, spas with radioactive waters that put flight to the most searing gout, plaguing doubt. An **androgyne** is an androgynous individual, possessing qualities of both sexes, that is: embodying the extremes of neither male nor female, but blending the two into a harmonious whole; a being of ambiguous gender.

Torpor in the Swing includes a walk-on part for a prepossessing androgyne who has a go at the heroine's anomie.[†] The author implies that she's overdosed on anodynes and plots a rude awakening in her bower of dappled light and silken screens.

"What I'm really looking for," said Flip, "is the embodiment of every promise running around loose on two more or less matching smooth or hairy legs: an androgyne who'll let me have my way when I don't know *what* I want, who'll keep me guessing when I do, who'll wear the skirt when I'm in the saddle and crack the whip when I've got the blues."

Is there no anodyne for this low-down, cussed feeling that I'm headed for annihilation, but with no oblivion in its wake?

antagonist
protagonist

An **antagonist** requires another to oppose, contend with in a struggle, battle of wits or wills: two antagonists make a fight. In literature, an *antagonist* is the principal opponent of the novel's or play's main character, its hero, heroine, or **protagonist**. Thus the morally ambiguous Reynaldo is the antagonist of Capriccio in *The Case of the Lapsed Credenza*, a novella based on the heroic high jinks of King Incognito VIII's right-hand man, who was, by the way, ambidextrous.

*O*ut of my way, you irrelevant quidnunc.[†] *I'm* the protagonist of this crime and romance thriller," said Drasko Mustafović in a rare flash of arrogance that bordered on hubris to a supernumerary with whom he shared an elevator ascending the Hotel Artaud.

In *The Espresso Murders,* Alfonsi Lombardini, accused of snuffing out eighteen intellectual drifters mid-cappuccino, confronts a formidable antagonist, Tanagra Canasta, whom he wins over to belief in his innocence once he's distracted her affection from one of the victims, a mustachioed poet of little promise and even less talent who'd lived in her mother's closet one bleak New England winter and emerged in the spring with a parody of *Paradise Lost* in macaronic language and a scarlet slipper clutched to his hypochondriacal chest.

"I never dreamed my own son might turn into an antagonist of breakers of the law," said one bandit to another as they discussed the woes of fatherhood and their bungled raid on the Schloss's vaults.

appraise
apprise

Appraise means to judge, weigh the worth of, evaluate, estimate. **Apprise** means to inform, give notice to, notify, and can also be spelled *apprize.*

*T*he trinkets were appraised at half their true value and tucked into a tube of antique circus posters headed down the river to St.-Eustache-on-Vye.

They hastened to apprise the debutante of her rights while she banged the mud off her dance floor heels and shook the sand and smudges out of her riven[†] ballgown.

"You apprise me of my rights and I'll commission a catalogue raisonné of your faux pas and fatal flaws," retorted the debutante with a presence of mind she'd acquired in her tête-à-tête with the troll.

He ran his hands along the filly's forequarters with the lingering touch of a veteran sensualist, then appraised her a probable descendant of Northern Lights, the stallion from a humble stable in the Vaasts of Laponesia.

apprehend
comprehend

Apprehend means to seize, capture, arrest, take into custody, and when applied to intellectual matters means to grasp or understand. It further means to become conscious of through the senses: to perceive. **Comprehend** means more specifically to understand.

*S*hall I apprehend these miscreants forthwith, or shall we let them carry on and do our bidding while they're at it? Common purposes can be found.

Do you still not comprehend the significance of the Samotrian invasion in the history of our beleaguered land?

"I'll *never* comprehend this ricocheting, rackety, rampageous language!" wailed Jonquil amid the din at the inn.

Although the jury of the Vast Monthrock Foundation did not fully comprehend Sigismund's proposal (and several members even doubted the existence or authenticity of *Gossamer and the Green Light*), they awarded her the grant anyway, since she'd applied for three years in a row, and the intensity of her obsession gave both her complexion and her prose a preternatural glow.

auspicious
propitious

Auspicious, of good omen, says that the time is right for success in the future—and implies importance, so that an auspicious occasion or moment is memorable in itself besides or instead of pointing to a happy outcome. **Propitious** offers favorable conditions on the spot, so that weather can be propitious for a picnic or travel, or a lovers' meeting or reconciliation can take place in propitious circumstances.

*I*t was an auspicious moment in the reign of Prolix I: henceforward, his succession would remain inviolate, his esteem intact.

"Not the most propitious setting for a tryst, is it?" asked Jonquil as the *compagnons*—proud, agile craftsmen—crawled in and out of their window at desperate intervals, bearing slabs of slate to and fro with an aimlessness that was all too evident in the jagged, ragged asymmetries of the roof atop the Schloss.

"Is this, or is it not, an auspicious sign?" asked General Ludović, having scanned the horizon and noticed a lone wolf lurching forward, then sideways, piercing the susurrus of card games and confessions in the camp's makeshift casino and chapel with an occasional agonized howl.

baleful
baneful

Although these are sometimes used interchangeably to mean menacing, pernicious, or harmful, **baneful**, meaning poisonous, is specifically applied to cases of toxicity. Thus it is often used for substances, causes, and influences that bring on death, as well as mere destruction. **Baleful** has a more foreshadowing quality in the evil it suggests, the malign influences it brings.

*T*he horizon greeted us with a baleful rumble of louring coruscations as we dreaded our way along the precipitous switchbacks of Upper Trajikistan.

It was rumored that Dariushka had been experimenting with baneful roots and plants in her studio for months before her fatal attack. Pages had found her tottering through remote hallways with her scalp, cuticles, and nostrils an electric purple, her frantic eyes sending out tracers of coppery red, tarnished silver and gold, her camisole awry and exposing her bosom, her smacking lips a lurid green.

Baleful looks were exchanged all around before someone gave the emergency button a thoughtful tap and brought down a squad of pacifists upon the incipient brawl.

blond
blonde

Blond is an adjective for either sex, and now and then it gets away from hair altogether to describe other materials. As a noun, it refers to a light-haired fellow. A **blonde** is a blond female, usually human, but in this book not necessarily.

$\mathcal{A}$fter you've bronzed and bouffanted those blotto sopranos," said Boris Marcelovsky to his assistants, a blond bombshell and a buxom blonde, "would you enamel the toes of those two Belladonni before they dismantle the magazine rack and otherwise trash my salon."

With his red mustache, blond sideburns, black eyebrows, and silver lining, General Pvbxtrz was a walking tapestry of all the genetic permutations ever visited upon his clan.

Nada Seria ran her hand over the blond wood surface of her desk and explained to Joubert early in their courtship that although she was of Magyar and Scandinavian extraction, she was only now, in her thirties and after multiple sex changes, turning from a blonde into a brunette.

born
borne

Since both words are past participles of *bear*,
you need to bear in mind which voice prevails
in a given instance: active or passive, that is.
Born is only for those to whom birth is given,
even if it seems like a struggle for both mother
and child.

*J*onquil was born in Blegue, but set off for Louvelandia when kicked out of Amplochacha U.

"Miss Mapp's charms have not gone unnoticed,
but I have borne her impertinence and sardonic
sotto voces with less indulgence than she as-
sumes," wrote the professor of her graduate
seminar on Balkan Trauma: A Truculent Topog-
raphy—and his objections were echoed throughout the department in which she'd blazed with
promise her sophomore and senior years (she
spent her junior year in Azuriko, High Albania,
and Laponesia, where she'd impressed one and
all with her courage and curiosity, her resilience
and instant acquisition of native ways).

careen
career

Careening can be more side to side in its hectic trajectory of progress, in keeping—or keeling—with its nautical origin. **Careering** hurtles headlong, at high speed, not necessarily out of control. Both words can mean more evenly to move forward at high speed. Natty Ampersand, an unflagging advocate of neglected words, calls attention to the underuse of **career**, noting that **careen** is often used where **career** would make as much, if not more, sense. "Probably because of how much easier it is to say **careen**, and fit other words around it, even in the mumbled silences of the writer's mouth," Ampersand suggests fragmentarily.

*C*areering along the autobahn toward Bluttenbad at three a.m., Jonquil, at the wheel of a silver Mercedes, was retracing in her mind the map the wizard had whispered beneath his parting, admonitory incantation.

Careening through the Schwarzwald was a zaftig[†] *Fräulein* named Hilda with a hamstrung faun panting in her wake and attempting to woo her in her native tongue, a Wagnerian orchestra hard at work in his imagination overwhelming each mispronunciation.

censer
censor
censure

Incense is burned in a **censer**, in holy or secular situations. To **censor** is to examine and expurgate letters or literature, removing or suppressing material deemed objectionable, whether it's suggestive, seditious, or otherwise too exciting. To **censure** is to criticize, condemn, express official disapproval of.

*S*aint Archulaga's nostrils twitched at the approaching censer; soon the tears were traveling down the ikon's cheeks and dropping into the hollows of her clavicles.

As she and the wizard had agreed, twice a week Jonquil shot off cryptograms which were impossible to censor or messages that revealed their true meaning only once they had been clipped of their various references to firebrands, phlebotomies, and moles.

Either we censure this smooth-talking Lavukistani upstart now or he'll soon be wagging his hindquarters through the empyrean and coaxing our susceptible queen into his wolf-drawn sylvan[†] sleigh.

ceremonial
ceremonious

These both relate to ceremonies, events or acts following formal rituals or customs, but **ceremonial** is more often applied to things (ceremonial raiments, tableware, headgear, accoutrements), and **ceremonious** to persons and things (an occasion, a venue, a hostess).

*I*f you're going to stand on ceremony in this raddled tearoom, Madame, then at least flash me your famous ceremonious grin while I tuck this rancid napkin under your chin.

On one of his rare, rushed visits home, Troto presented his sweetheart, Milanka, with a ceremonial dagger that the Samotrian empire's army had plundered during a foray at the Donutrian court.

Jesperanda, clad from head to foot in full ceremonial splendor, entered the ballroom with her epic poem tucked into a sturdy sheath where usually a saber would rattle.

She had composed this recollection of rapacious misdeeds and romantic pursuits for the ceremonious occasion of honoring recently wounded soldiers and pinning more gaudy medals on the frock coats of the generals.

> **Ceremonious** can also imply an overwrought display, an absurd degree of etiquette or formality, as if affectation had taken over the arrangements and presentation.

*F*orks were wielded with the stateliness usually reserved for royal scepters; introductions were made with such gravity that a name was not merely a name, or even a pedigree. In short," summed up the social columnist for the *Passevitza Clarion,* "the guests felt compelled to conduct themselves like cadavers on parole, and a ceremonious time was had by all till some stole off to Les Trottoirs de Buenos Aires to jostle their blood and warm their bones."

chicanery
duplicity

While these both involve deception, **duplicity** implies double-dealing, and **chicanery** suggests slyness, wiliness, and trickery.

*C*apriccio may be capricious, but he hasn't a duplicitous bone in his skull," avouched Ilona's maid-in-waiting while suspicions slithered and surged at court and amplified abroad.

Duplicity is as common among drug lords as honor is among thieves.

"I'm afraid we've fallen for a bit of very professional chicanery here," said the butler to himself and the coronated head of mutton delivered by Zupervol Express.

Was Alabastro ever apprised of his wife's duplicity? Her docile mien on state occasions, her exquisite bedtime manners—then playing footsy with the devil, coquetting about with fiends.

climactic
climatic

Climactic: *climax*
Climatic: *climate*

> Zoë Platgut prefers to keep her mouth shut
> when she discusses these two, and uses the
> blackboard, a laptop, paper airplane, or pan-
> tomime (which often obscures the issue, as
> both words find her fanning herself and panting
> most volubly). I therefore have honored her
> schematics on this theme: see above.

*T*oo many climactic moments for even a fifty-act
opera," might Moltgang have written after the
opening, but his true thoughts we shall never
hear.

Climatic changes and extremes are definitely in
the cards with the resurgence of the rubicund[†]
current in the Samotrian Sea, the eruption of
Mount Placido, the erratic posturings of ermines
and wolves.

> Then there's **climacteric**, which also finds Zoë
> fanning herself and popping estrogen, as its
> culmination is menopause. More generally, it
> means any critical stage or period. As an
> adjective, it means critical or crucial.

*T*he coroner offered a three-pronged explanation for Dariushka's demise:

  1—frenzy brought on by her Hungarian dancing master
  2—a sudden, urgent longing for Eternity
  3—premature climacteric hot flash combustion / meltdown

collude
connive

Both these words mean to scheme, to plot, conspire, to act secretly or underhandedly for fraudulent or illegal purpose. **Connive** takes off on its own in meaning to look the other way while knowing what's going on, to imply encouragement or assent by feigning ignorance.

*C*ome over to this corner and collude with me, baby" was an overused come-on of Prolix X, whose conspiracies never went past dalliance and whose ministers were the most upright in the history of the realm.

By contrast, Prolix XI, his son, contrived his own spectacular downfall after years of conniving with bureaucratic crooks.

The brigands with fans have been colluding against local officials with a band of slaphappy vandals the *Passevitza Clarion* has inaccurately dubbed their Doppelgäng. In fact, the true Doppelgäng is elsewhere engaged, marauding the countryside of Lavukistan with Belle Époque fans in their fluttering hands and garters over their alpenstocks.

"Your connivance will take you far—into exile, that is," predicted Incognito VI to his heir as he foresaw each possible failing.

complacent
complaisant

Complaisant means eager to please, and if such eagerness leads to success, it can also lead to complacency, which could drift into laziness. **Complacent** means pleased with oneself, self-satisfied, with a surfeit of contentment (not very motivating).

*A*fter consuming several strudels and Sacher tortes, Pasha Partout would grow even more complacent than usual and loll upon his cushions in a majestic stupor while his playmates mugged him of his favorite magazines, abandoned puzzles, and multilingual talking dolls.

In the first years of her marriage, Dariushka struck most who shook her hand or snapped her picture as a complaisant companion for King Alabastro and a photogenic pinup for both homesick soldiers and diplomats' concubines, but as her character acquired dimension, her interests, entourage, and charisma grew apace, and the mask of legend seized her face.

"You'll not catch me growing complacent after my first hostile takeover and the ruination of Lavukistan's disabled dynasties," Trill assured his mentor, Moostracht, who was the next on his list to roll.

congenial
congenital

Congenial describes an attitude, manner, almost a state of grace in this age of suspicion and spite: it means affable, friendly, hospitable, warm-hearted, complaisant, always welcome at a party. **Congenital** means from birth, if not before it, or by nature, inherent, so it can apply to physical conditions, characteristics, and temperament. To open "Up Your Eponym," Startling Glower was introduced as "our congenital host" on a special program of misdemeanors and malapropisms.

*W*hat phosphorescent big teeth you have! What wild eyes! What a battered yet luxuriant fur coat you are wearing! What a congenial companion I shall make of you! And you will shatter my sleep and foreshadow my sempiternal[†] night.

Are those flashing teeth congenital, or are they the result of your experience in this wayward, wacky habitat—or several expensive sessions with a demon dentist?

This flutter is congenital: she's been batting her eyes since she was in the cradle, and many a curious creature has she attracted thereby.

Jonquil may be amiable in fits and starts, but she is also congenitally contentious.

conjure

Is it **conjure** or **conjure up**? This was the subject
of a knee play inserted quite deftly (thanks to
the choreography of Manx Vulpino) into an
episode of "Up Your Eponym." The consensus
of the motley band in heated argument
(dragged in from the avenida and academia):
When it means to call up, call forth, bring on,
bring into existence or one's presence (as if by
magic), it takes *up,* as it does when it means to
bring to mind, to recall. One of the kidnapped
guests turned out to be a genuine conjure man
from the deep South (a frequent visitor chez
Drat Siltlow's three great-aunts; when he
showed up for Drat's thirteenth birthday, he
changed the lad's voice with a flap of his dirty
handkerchief, and conjured a birthday cake
from the devil's own pastry chef—but more
about that later!) who spirited the program off
to another television studio where they were
taping a soap set in Louvelandia.

Conjure can also mean to beg, implore, appeal
to someone.

I conjure you, oh do desist from these reckless
speculations and ancient calumnies!" pleaded
Angie Canasta of Rafael Todos los Muertos as
the interview entered its darkest hour.

continual
continuous

A difference does indeed divide these two. My esteemed colleague has assured me in both writing and pantomime that this is so. In fact, at the end of his performance, Fossilblast pulled out of a rabbit-fur top hat a palimpsest[†] from the royal library of the Incognito succession that demonstrates the two in action. **Continual**: in rapid succession or recurrence, or else, when apt, ongoing; **continuous**: constant, uninterrupted.

*C*ontinual trips to the fountain failed to slake her thirst or lower her temperature, so Dariushka caught on fire," the court physician surmised.

"Continual pedaling up gentle inclines is endangering Incognito's hip sockets, but his knees are in delectable shape!" exclaimed the king's private rheumatologist over a platter of oysters and indiscretions recorded by a barnacle on a plaster of Paris mermaid's midriff (part of the decor).

"Continuous and even continual entertainment leads to attrition[†] of the imagination," concluded the study of four-, fourteen-, and forty-year-olds commissioned by Prolix IX, a fanatical patron of the arts.

"Continuous exposure to the media will soon send them all away," hypothesized Dariushka thirty-eight hours into her balcony marathon of mooning, mating calls of tropical birds, and mathematical tricks worthy of the humblest idiot savant.

could of
could have

> Although Drat Siltlow grew up with **could of**, and although Zoë Platgut can quote with approximate body language most of Marlon Brando's monologues by heart, including his "I coulda been a contender" speech in *On the Waterfront*, both concede that it's supposed to be **could have**, even though when said out loud, it often slurs into the easier elision.

I could have made a whopping profit out of that lost cause if you'd just faxed me the details overnight," Trill Apasaguena fired off to one of his acolytes[†] up the creek in Azuriko.

"You could have been more considerate of my claustrophobia when you abandoned me among those aggressive elbows and heavy breathers in the Quisisana Arcade," Odious wrote in a re-

proachful note to Cassandra, who had other mirrors to read.

council
counsel

A council is a deliberative body of people
assembled to act in some advisory or authorita-
tive capacity.

$\mathcal{T}$he Council of Pakriatz met to deliberate one
more endless round about the parking situation
beneath the city center, where a color-blind attendant enforced a color-coded pattern of movement and placement, regardless of the relative
volumes of reds, creams, silver greys, blues and
greens, yellow roundabouts, and black limou-
sines.

Counsel as a noun is guidance or advice; as a
verb it's giving them.

I counsel you to sleep on it, pal, and forget you
ever told me," said Serafima Dos Equis to Dante
Kaputo, who was finding that establishing an
alibi was as elusive an enterprise as tracking
down Dusty Saxon.

The council will reconvene first thing next week if Alabastro remains besotted with grief and dripping with diamonds and lace.

The cartographer counseled not taking these accounts too literally, Trajikistan being nothing if not subjective: tragedy in the eye of the traveler.

decry
descry

> To **decry** is to belittle, denounce, deprecate, or disparage openly. To **descry** is to discern something difficult to catch sight of (often from a distance) or to discover by careful observation.

*J*acomino Vervazzo flowed through the country on a streamlined barge decrying the tawdry architecture and cutthroat construction within sight of the River Logomachia.

"What a tinseled mouthful of ravening aspersions," decried Poco Rabinowitz after Gavril Dark had harangued and appeased the nation.

I varnished my eyelashes and ironed my nylons in hopes that the lord chamberlain would not descry my humble, illegitimate origins and my rusticated patois and contours.

From the edge of the precipice Jonquil descried a feather of hope in the shape of a man-hunting eagle.

degenerate
deteriorate

As a verb, **degenerate** is more apt for character issues—to describe in active fashion the loss or lessening of virtue. Note its use below as a noun (one who has degenerated or is showing great promise in that direction). **Deteriorate** is more simply a matter of wearing out, losing vitality or strength, falling into shambles.

*H*is hip sockets will deteriorate over time, so you should bring him in for a biannual checkup," cautioned the doctor to the dentist while the robot amused himself in the corridor with his new dancing shoes and a cassette of the great Gardel on the Walkman installed in his solar plexus—his analogue of a heart.

"Our courtiers have degenerated into a shabby rabble of syphilitic sybarites wrapped in fur coats and Turkish towels," read an attack in the *Darkling Mirror,* which was airing choleric views on everything from mud baths to corruption of the clergy during the first week of spring.

"I was counting on my son to be a degenerate, and instead he's become a smooth-shaven constable with a winsome moue[†] and shiny buttons, immaculate record, and solemn vows he keeps because he doesn't know what they mean," lamented a disappointed paterfamilias into a sympathetic ear.

demur
demure

To **demur** is to voice opposition, to object, often to delay decision or action. **Demure** means modest, shy, or reserved in manner, behavior, sometimes affectedly so.

*N*o no no no no," demurred Despina, "I am not just now at your behest or beckoning: I have quandaries to ponder, and telegrams to dispatch."

"Demure in demeanor, diabolical in effect" is how Jonquil's second grade teacher summed up her character in the behavior report for that *annus horribilis* of our errant heroine.

deprecate
deprecate

> To **deprecate** is to heap with scorn, aspersions, disapproval; to deplore; to belittle. To **depreciate** is to lessen in price or value—transitively or intransitively. Less often, it means to belittle, or deprecate.

*E*ver quick to deprecate what he couldn't understand, Bottie, feeling bellicose, called the choreography belletristic,[†] the music narcissistic, the lighting fidgety and arcane, and yet he wooed the entire corps de ballet, having divided and conquered them with one bouquet.

"Well, naturally, our coffins depreciate over time, but that's partly the fault of the corpse, decomposing with no decency or decorum after all our ministrations and cosmetic considerations," warbled the master of cerements[†] at Chichikov & Company to a bereaved and bartering bride.

He began by deprecating the condition of the roads, the precipitous passes and cantankerous crags, then praised to the heavens the Inn of Serenity and Iniquity with its view of Mount Mousserousque and a library of erotica tucked into the honor bars of its X-rated suites.

"Wanhope Castle would normally depreciate over time, but because it is haunted, we can amortize the ghost and invest some capital in repairs to offset any deteriorations," says Antonio, staggering through a patch of real estate jargon in *Giovanna's Mortgage*.

discreet
discrete

Discreet means prudent, tactful, careful in judgment, usually about keeping something quiet, hidden, under wraps, private—best not revealed. It becomes *discretion* in the act of becoming a noun, *indiscretion* in the act of becoming a blunder, error in judgment, lapse in vigilance or tact.

*J*onquil, accustomed to making her way with insolence, impertinence, intemperance, and impulsiveness, was not totally without insight and savoir-vivre. After a few close calls, she realized that to come out of Trajikistan alive, she would have to be both circumspect and discreet.

Katya began slipping up in matters that required discretion, so Jacaranda persuaded the butler to administer a timid spanking without removing his gloves, and the wayward soubrette also received a mild reproof in her own handwriting as dictated by Mustafović himself in his suite at Hotel Artaud.

"Any more indiscretions in your casual allusions and handling of cash, and you'll be hounding the joyless streets for other employment," said Constanza to Nada Seria, who'd dropped a hint about an irascible cavalier while her mistress was out of temper.

> **Discrete** means separate, distinct, and in its rare appearances as a noun, it makes them as *discreteness*.

*A*ddressing himself to the question of a discrete hiding place for his wad of treasure, Pasha Partout roused himself at last one late afternoon from a luscious loll and prodded it into the midst of a zaftig† cushion that only he was allowed to approach or touch.

"The orgy in the *grand salon* tonight shall consist of five discrete movements, or courses, if you

will," adumbrated Amaranthia to an odd assortment of overnight guests—all cellists, composers, or chefs.

In the catacombs you will find discrete niches where vanquished vandals have stashed their plunder in the course of stealing away; family crypts from the Alabastro succession; a touching memento to the little princess Celestina (a lock of hair tied with a strip of Samotrian silk, her supple fishing rod, the salamander she used to nap with on the riverbank, and wreaths of various indigenous flowers); the bones of ancient outlaws and animals and a sled of Prolix IX; many bottles of fine wines and brandies disguised as nuclear waste; the Countess of Troo's collection of shoes; and a dark mirror that's never been faced.

disinterested
uninterested

If, in making a decision or judgment, you are **disinterested**, you have not been bought off, you're impartial, unbiased, you have no vested interest: a fine condition in which to make a cool appraisal. If you are **uninterested** in something, you are indifferent, teetering on the brink of boredom: it does not rouse your interest.

*W*ithin sixteen months, drama critic Frodo Asgard of the *Darkling Mirror* evolved from disinterested aesthete to manacled, beholden hack.

"Throw in your dishtowel, you retrograde roustabout, and take a disinterested shuffle through the Seven Deadly Virtues with my svelte soubrette and me," said Yolanta to the tarted-up bartender on the outs with his boyfriend, Flip.

Uninterested in all his subjects over the age of seventeen, Incognito X was ousted by an unlikely alliance of frauds and fanatics, chorus girls and sober citizens, breadwinners from the inner cities, hinterlands, and suburban sprawls—and was replaced by an upstart from an obscure offshoot of the family: the steady, the stolid Queen Maud.

disparate
desperate

Disparate means utterly distinct, different, dissimilar. **Desperate** takes care of a gamut of emotional extremes: hopeless, despairing, in dire, urgent need, even driven to violence.

*D*isparate springs bubbling forth from nowhere are but the beginnings of Azuriko's bounteous rivers and streams, and one geopoetic monograph insinuates that the country has for centuries tapped into sources beneath neighboring countries as well as the bottomless lake in Blegue. Single-cell mutants and larger aquatic creatures unique to Azuriko have turned up on bikinis worn in Lake Quisisana, as have various bloated corpses that once were guests at the Schloss.

"Curiously, my attraction to him is both desperate and serene," wrote Jonquil in her journal before more incendiary looks were exchanged.

In matching getups of storm-tossed tulle, the two runaways from the seraglio, Fatima and Patina, discussed their desperate plight and daring plans (to open a chain of pajama boutiques in Amplochacha, Evrique, Oostricht, and Baudine) as they paced the decks of the *Scarlatina* on its outward-bound journey from Constantinople.

The design for Todor's headstone elicited disparate aesthetic interpretations from various members of the clan, who pronounced it, in one riposte amidst another, Bogomil Bauhaus, Confectionery of the Khazars, and Byzantine Bosch—before the slivovitz and sausages ensnared their tongues in poetry and poetics and their women, weary of having heard it all before, delivered mock-heroic monologues along with flying plates and cups.

The desperate criminals were brought to justice in a curious way: all their sons turned out O.K.

displace
misplace

When an object or loved one is **displaced**, it has shifted or been shifted permanently (more or less) from the place it's accustomed to occupy. When the same thing or person is **misplaced**, it has wandered off or been abducted to some wrong place, where it might cause frustration if someone's looking for it where it usually is or where he/she thinks it should be. In certain instances *misplaced* is synonymous with *mislaid*.

*D*isplaced Bosoxians wandered the earth with woe weighing down their diminished possessions and uncertainty heightening their grief.

"I've misplaced my baby!" wailed Dodeska, scattering hysteria through the Quisisana Arcade and up and down the esplanade.

Wanted: displaced persons from all walks of life to fill hundreds of dead men's shoes.

"I don't mean to displace you, sir," said Jonquil, settling down with misgivings and exchanging dark, piercing glances with a gallant gadabout glad to give up his seat in the third-class coach heading up the ravine.

Sonia Tweazle Scronx was feeling misplaced as nanny to Pasha Partout, whose behavior defied descriptions in all the manuals for a dragon of his age.

distinct
distinctive

When an object or creature is **distinct**, it stands out ("But not because it's eccentric!" bellow all six of my eccentric authorities at once), is recognizable in a crowd; it proclaims itself. When a quality or attribute is **distinctive**, it helps us distinguish one thing from another, renders it recognizable.

A distinctive element of the Schloss is the secret underground passage connecting it to the dead center of Amplochacha: the mausoleum of the royal family with its aggressive and importunate ghosts.

The three Saturnine Yet Oversexed Sisters create a distinct silhouette at dawn and in the savage twilight when you are looking toward the desolate region of Fingblat.

"I thought I detected a distinct trace of irony in that finance minister's minion's monologue," Serafima Dos Equis wrote to his superior from the spa in Trajikistan. As his own edges were blurring there along with the others', he couldn't quite trust his senses.

> A frequently used term in the Missing Persons Bureau, on mug shot Wanted posters, is **distinguishing features**: those features by which one might distinguish a person, those features that render him or her more distinct—that is, distinctive!

*T*roto Asfoblatz
Height: 2 meters
Weight: 81 kilos
Hair: None (except in his nostrils and ears; see also eyes)
Eyes: Gunmetal grey with lashes 1 centimeter in length
Distinguishing features:
An Orthodox cross tattooed onto sole of left foot, removable upper left molar, 7 toes on right foot, extra navel beside the usual one
A distinctive, lurching gait apparent especially from a distance

drunk
drunken

This is partly a mere matter of position. As Drat Siltlow explains, "**Drunken** is the adjective that can only precede the noun (i.e., the person who is inebriated—or, in Baudelaire's case, the tipsy vessel), while **drunk** is the one that follows a verb: we got drunk on slivovitz and carried on till dawn / he stayed drunk for the next two days while I mucked about on the verandah." There is an exception to this pattern that has crept in through the law, and that is in the terms *drunk driver* and *drunk driving,* as the Schloss's au pair will demonstrate below.

*F*lip was drunk when he got rumbled on the barroom floor, so he came out of the fracas perplexed and dazed, bruised and ashamed, but practically unscathed.

A drunken debutante and an upright troll confronted the officer with unblinking eyes and an otherworldly sang-froid.[†]

At the bottom of the Bay of Oublanskaia lies the evidence of doomed voyages: carcasses of drunken boats, toppled yachts, and travelers who could neither swim nor flap their water wings.

Hauled in for drunk driving without a license, Katya was released to the care of her protector, thanks not only to his powerful connections but also to the lowdown he had on various chief inspectors.

emigrate
immigrate

> To leave one's country in a very serious way, perhaps permanently, is to **emigrate**. When one fixes on settling in a strange new country, one **immigrates** there, as an immigrant.

*N*o one has ever successfully immigrated to Lavukistan. It's far too patronizing and phlebotomic in its red-tape chicaneries and day-to-day treatment of transients and deracinated[†] survivors.

Emigrations—and escapes—from Bosoxia were manifold during the years of Samotrian hegemony.[†]

"We fled the country when we heard what was happening at Bluttenbad, taking only our leotards, tights, toe shoes, and tennis rackets (picking up alarm clocks for symbolic, not time-telling, purposes as we skulked through Amplochacha in the dead of night), and by the grace of God, on fake passports, we journeyed to a distant land with intentions to immigrate once a cousin there could secure through hidden connections our fast-forward imprimatur,"[†] explained Kamila on behalf of Ladislas, Toosla, and Laslo to Rafael Todos los Muertos, who'd tracked them down and was conducting an elusive interview by phone.

> An *emigré*, as celebrated in Youssou N'Dour's CD *Emigrés*, is a person who must leave his country for political, martial, or otherwise desperate and despondent reasons. An *emigrant* leaves less traumatically.

eremitic
hermetic

Eremitic is the adjective belonging to a hermit, especially a religious recluse. **Hermetic** is related to Hermes, and means so completely sealed that no air can enter (when applied to a container) or impervious to outside influences. Its other realm is the occult, where it pertains to magic and alchemy.

*M*y dears! The decor has gone positively eremitic!" exclaimed Lady Gallimauf to Jesperanda and Miranda, recounting her first visit to Count Ghastly since his depression had caved him in.

King Alabastro kept Dariushka's eyeballs and heart in a hermetically sealed bivalve coffer, her garter belt entwined with his suspenders, her finger cymbals with his cuff links, and her slingback satin slippers at the foot of their conjugal bed.

Todor's clan dwelt in a hermetic cleft of a mountain ("rather like an eyrie," thought Jonquil when she passed through during her junior year abroad) from which they made their forays onto villagers and wayfarers far below.

"That clique is strictly for seekers of a hermetic persuasion," cautioned the footman during another clandestine tutorial with his alchimerical queen.

exacerbate
exasperate

> To **exacerbate** is to make worse by increasing degree of severity, violence, bitterness. To **exasperate** is to try the patience of, to push to the limit, to infuriate or irritate, throw into a state of annoyed frustration.

ook, don't exacerbate the situation by swallowing suicide pills," pleaded the Grim Reaper of the baba, who was keeping him on his Cartesian toes through such ingenious games and gambits that he couldn't bear the thought of losing her.

"It was exasperating! All those extras expecting triple-star treatment and carte blanche† carousals after the shoot," roared director Tyger Mischief about filming the fulminating crowd scenes in *Out of the Loud Hound of Darkness* with its population gone berserk and in thrall of the thrilling creature.

fatal
fateful

A **fateful** event cries out "Destiny!" or conjures a turning point. "It is meant to be," one might say, and it means so much that all—or something—is changed from that moment forward, hence it means momentous. A **fateful** moment or event affects or determines one's fate or future. On a casual basis, **fatal** is used synonymously with this word when applied to slices of time: a fatal moment, a fateful day, the fatal hour—all carry much the same significance. But let's get serious. A **fatal** dose, step, strategy, deception, alliance, attraction can kill you quite literally or figuratively—at the very least cause a downfall or disaster, as in a fatal mistake.

*J*onquil and Drasko exchanged their first fateful glance in a mirror over a row of keys to the inn's chatterbox, prayer, and map rooms. "The rapture we bring to each other's faces" is how Jonquil recorded in her journal that moment of lost-and-found-again déjà vu.

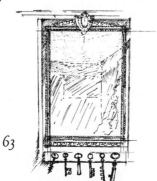

"Oh, fatal day! Why, oh why did I decide that afternoon to indulge my fancy for a saunter through the arcade?" lamented Dodeska to her sister, who was offering long-distance commiseration and suggesting she look into adopting some of Rumania's many orphans.

Sharply before his dishonorable demise,* Vast Monthrock established a foundation for writers of belletristic† bellicosity and insupportable hypotheses.

The first fatal attack at the Palaz of Hoon had nothing to do with the Belladonna Mafia. The prank of a teenage terrorist from Morski, it ironically saved many lives, for the place cleared out in seconds flat after the combustion of Vast Monthrock. By the time the Mafiosi's bomb went off, there remained on the premises only a few lower life forms and two health inspectors, all having a nosh in the pantry.

It was a fateful trip Trill Apasaguena made to the Vaasts of Laponesia, where, on a misguided sartorial quest, he inadvertently acquired the racehorse that would sire a fortune in his stables.

* ingestion of a fatal cookie—it exploded—at the Palaz of Hoon

64

foray
fray
affray

> These can be quite rough experiences. A **foray** is
> a quick raid, often for plunder, or a sudden and
> rapid attack. In the marketplace or other
> theaters of competition, it is an initial venture.
> As a verb, **foray** means to maraud, to invade; or
> to ravage, pillage for plunder.

*T*he foray that began at Ambukavatz (nothing
much of value there besides one fabulous private collection of blues records and a watch that
tells the time according to Samotrian calcula-
tions) continued till the scattered soldiers recon-
vened at Café Sans-Culottes et Compagnie and
swapped mendacities.

"You boys go out there and foray for a few hours
to get it out of your systems, but I want you all in
bed by ten," said General Pvbxtrz to a few aimless
stragglers still under his command but in danger
of succumbing to a wave of anomie.[†]

His foray on the racetrack with Northern Lights
quickened Trill's pulse and took his mind far
from the saddening shroud he'd been offered by
a Trajik tailor in an auroral reverie.

> A **fray** is a fight, skirmish, or battle; a sporting
> competition or contest; a noisy quarrel or
> brawl. An **affray** is a public fight; a noisy quarrel;
> a brawl, fracas.

$\mathcal{S}$oundly acquitting himself in the fray among the
fens of Fingblat, Troto serenaded his sweetheart
with cassettes of epic poems recounting his val-
orous deeds and reviling his oligarchic foes.

The affray at Blotto Junction could have followed
a much bloodier scenario had Ziggie Spurthrast
not appeared in her leopard-skin getup and shot
down a row of whisky bottles with the revolver
she'd acquired in a poker game with a passenger
they'd taken on in Patagonia.

> **Fray** as a verb means to cause to ravel or
> unravel, undo at the ends; to discompose,
> upset.

$\mathcal{M}$y nerves are frayed, and you're smearing my
makeup and fraying my silk kimono!" yapped
Zap to Rip, who wasn't called that for nothing.

"It was, when all was said and undone, a di-
sheveling, fraying experience," wrote Troto to Milanka about an ambush that left many of his

fellow soldiers flayed or else drowned in the fens of Fingblat.

forceful
forcible

Force is evident in both words, a force so great it can lull us into thinking them synonymous. But taking a **forceful** position on the razing of a derelict hotel does not necessarily involve dynamite and bulldozers on one side or Molotov cocktails and hostage-taking on the other: it means merely a strong stand, which could be entirely verbal—eloquent, adamant, and direct. **Forcible** does put across the idea of action by physical force.

*F*amous for his forcible entries and invisible exits, Serafima Dos Equis shattered his way into the crystal castle and slipped an ultimatum onto the breakfast tray of the heir apparent, later known as Vanya the Bald.

Knowing they could rely on Frotteau Dessange to forcefully introduce a touchy subject, Trill's staff hauled him in by the scruff of his neck and injected his gibbering, ghoulish voice into the dreary deliberations of the boardroom.

She was forceful through and through, and Ziggie Spurthrast lapped up the accolades her antics inspired among the *Scarlatina*'s crew and passengers and the creatures of the deep blue sea.

Forcibly sequestering the feistier brigands in his mountain fastness (the name of the mountain keeps its secret to this day), Drasko Mustafović pocketed the key and set off for his assignation with the impetuous, luminescent Katya.

forgo
forego

To **forgo** is to deprive oneself of, to abstain from, relinquish. To **forego** is to precede, as in time or place. This is also an alternative spelling of *forgo*, with that sense of deprivation, abstinence, or renunciation. But *forgo* never means to precede, to go before.

$\mathcal{P}$lease, give me some real insights next time, and not just a concatenation of these obvious, foregone conclusions," said the telegram Serafima was handed as he asked for his room key and one of the hotel trollops.

If the foregoing is true, if you can sail clear of perjury, please sign on the broken line and kiss the portrait of our bedizened monarch by Ambruto Trabosie.

"I'm willing to forgo a picnic with the footmen and alchemist if you'll house the victims of Mount Placido's eruption in those barracks at Baudine," bartered the bride of Alabastro, a girl from the restive provinces herself who'd lost her favorite uncles to a temperamental scree.*

* scree: a steep mass of loose rock on a mountainside; talus

fortuitous
fortunate

A **fortunate** occurrence brings fortune—thanks to the benevolent machinations of luck. In hallowed, austere tradition (as opposed to its freewheeling use for implying a *happy* accident, a felicitous fluke), **fortuitous** means merely happening by chance or accident, with either welcome or deleterious consequences.

*T*he fortuitous anchor-dropping of the *Scarlatina* off Patagonia (it was *supposed* to be going through the Panama Canal) decided Torquil's next move: he threw in the towel on his waitressing gig (he'd found that working in drag significantly augmented his tips) and put his fate in the capricious hands of the fetching second mate.

"How fortunate that my uncle Ladislas was on the Nismer–East Blagundia express that day and avoided the catastrophe!" continued Dariushka, reminiscing about the loss of her other uncles.

"Count yourself fortunate you weren't born in a distant century if a sight like this sets your teeth chattering," said Despina to Saskiak, who was having some trouble with the skeleton.

A fortuitous meeting of two banditti on the mountain pass would seriously rumple the next wayfarers' reservations at the Inn of Serenity and Iniquity up ahead.

"Well! Wasn't that a bit of fortuitous hindsight!" says Giovanna malappropriately in the story of her unfortunate mortgage.

founder
flounder

Founder means to sink, collapse, fail utterly, bomb. **Flounder**, on the other hand, presents quite a kinetic picture: flailing arms, thrashing about, so it's to move, react, proceed with awkward uncertainty or clumsy confusion. If all this is ineffectual, *foundering* may be one's fate.

The project foundered while still a proposal, so Trill fired off a fax to Nimbo Moostracht beseeching a few words of encouragement and a check to start a new venture.

Jonquil never floundered in any of her courses, but her saucy manner and mere presence was such a subversive catalyst in any classroom that her professors arranged two-week field trips every other month to defuse the explosive situation and throttle her seditious influence out on the open range.

"She's so afraid of foundering before final exams that she's given up attending class to stay in bed and study," wrote Nola's father to her first grade teacher, keeping his child to himself and continuing with her lessons in Old Norse and Provençal before a total immersion in the language of her contemporaries reduced her brain to fever.

fury
furor

Yes, **furor**, like **fury**, can mean anger or a state of intense excitement or frenzy, but it's also a great commotion or public uproar.

*W*hat a furor an ill-timed announcement can unleash! What a pandemonium in the mittel-platzen!" read the twin headlines in the *Alsmeer Eventual* and the *Lumbachen Reminder*.

"Is this fury or is it madness?" Torquil finally asked himself halfway to Patagonia.

"What I'd like to see is a little furor in this sleepy town, and up the skirts of Dusty Saxon," wrote Dante Kaputo, aware that this could be read in at least two ways, on the wall of the Ministry of Sports and Leisure.

gambit
gamut

> A **gambit** is a ploy, any maneuver used to gain advantage; a remark made to open or redirect a conversation. A **gamut** is an entire range or extent, a full spectrum.

I'm not falling for that gambit!" scribbled Count Ghastly on the windowpane and still refusing to speak.

"He's halfway through the gamut of his usual evasiveness," commented Miranda, who'd been through this farce twice before and was looking after the Labradors.

Over Kristiana's face rippled a gamut of rabid emotions that only the panther could interpret.

gesticulation
gesture

> A **gesticulation** is a more exaggerated, even flailing use of appendages than is usually engaged in a **gesture**.

Mind your gesticulations, darling, or you'll call unwanted attention to our collusive sortie with a coup d'état at its apogee.[†]

"Is that an obscene gesture where you come from, or is it a Freudian flip of your scythe?" queried the baba on her third rum and bracing herself for an all-nighter of coquetry and black-humored badinage.

He stood there on the platform gesticulating wildly as the train roared past the station of East

Pakriatz, hell-bent for the conductor's blind date with a travel/secret agent in the no man's land of southwestern Lavukistan.

glance
glimpse

A **glance** captures more than a **glimpse**, although both are brief, quick views of something. A *glance* at a corner of a garden party may provide only a *glimpse* of the deadly dahlias. A *glimpse* is so rapid that not all of the object or person may be taken in, whereas one might well say "She took all of him in with a single glance." As verbs, these words continue this distinction, but *glance* takes no object as it looks quickly, while *glimpse* does: We glanced at each other, then away. I glimpsed a scintilla of concupiscence in his averted face. *Glances* are taken; *glimpses* are caught.

*D*o you have time to glance over these figures and see if I've made any egregious errors?" Trill asked his chief accountant during a week of cat-and-mouse, which he'd sometimes play to test his employees' integrity and accuracy of vision.

"I swear, I caught only a glimpse of her face in a train compartment full of cigar smokers, and she was wearing huge fox fur gloves and an amorphous[†] hooded garment that obscured her swiveling profile," said the sniveling guttersnipe who'd been stealing passports from the couchettes until he was kidnapped into a private investigation.

"The horror! The horror! And such vanity, too!" pronounced Boris Marcelovsky, purveying the morning's gossip—the fate of a colleague of his who had displeased a Belladonna Mafiosa. "She took a quick glance at herself in the mirror and then she fired the revolver."

We barely glimpsed the flashing teeth and rush of darkness that announced the creature's evanescence.

She polished her contours and powdered her appendages in hopes that one day a gloaming glance from him would alight on her body.

And here we have a metaphoric spin on the verb **glance**:

*T*he rock glanced off the surface with six ga-zelleschaft leaps before plunging into the fath-omless waters of Lake Sandali, the twin sister of Lake Shayesteh.

grateful
gratified

When one is **grateful**, one is full of gratitude, appreciation of kindness and generosity: thankful, even much obliged if one has such score-keeping tendencies. *Gratification* comes from pleasure: it's satisfaction with a sensuous twist, the upshot of being indulged, so **gratified** describes a delectable state, whether it applies to a physical sensation or the frisson brought on by a compliment.

*G*rateful, but beyond consolation, Alabastro sat in bed shredding his letters of condolence, then re-combining the myriad fragments and phrases into exquisite cadaverish messages to be scat-tered with his consort's ashes.

"I am most gratified by this award and the honor it bespeaks," wrote Sigismund Lolotte Flint-Page to the Vast Monthrock Foundation on receiving word of her next two years of material comfort and enslavement.

Most guests left the Schloss exhausted and disheveled, but with senses and appetites they didn't even know they had either gratified or roused from a regrettable slumber.

grievous
grieving
grief-stricken

> Something that's **grievous** causes pain, heartache, anguish, grief. A person who's been dealt a *grievous* blow or served some woeful tidings would be **grief-stricken** and, in more active mode, **grieving**.

$\mathcal{T}$he Bosoxian refugees suffered grievous emotional injury from their wrenching physical displacements and the evils that had ravaged their homeland over a question of hegemony.[†]

The grief-stricken Dodeska caught glimpses of her lost child wherever she went, and it was only after a small body with the family teeth washed up on the shore that she gave full vent to her grieving.

The grieving rats tarried long after the mass funeral and official period of mourning in Louvelandia, and soon begot several new generations of healthy, rapacious offspring.

historic
historical

Yes, these both have to do with history and swap places from time to time, crossing over the fine line of distinction that Glower illuminates thusly: "If some thing, person, place is noted for its association with some thing, person, event in history, it's **historic**: a historic battleground, war cry, edifice, monument, boulevard, personage, document, treaty, disaster, urban revamping, art movement, missile launching, speech, telegram, exposé of spy ring, etc."

*A*nother historic must-see in the back streets of Eloria is the hovel where Trill Apasaguena dwelt in destitution and unspeakable squalor before roving capitalist Nimbo Moostracht discovered his hidden entrepreneurial potential (not to mention his innate sense of style) and sent him to Blegue's finest business academy to tauten him up and flex the financial acumen that would one day leave economists speechless and many corporations facing death.

It was during this time that Blegue signed its historic peace and trade pact with affluent Azuriko, which would triple Trill's empire in the years to come.

The historic journey undertaken by a febrile and contumacious royal pack rat required a convoy of coaches to draggle her frou-frou, autograph albums, pharmacopoeia, and bric-a-brac through the countryside of her maternal granny's fabled escapades.

> **Historical** doesn't imply importance in the big picture of human chronology: it's for whatever once existed, whether important or incidental in the past (e.g., the minor historical figure Sasboom Van Trotta; a historical exploration, expedition)—although it's sometimes applied to things of significance, and also to things concerned with history or study of the past, such as a historical novel, society, or museum.

Out of the Loud Hound of Darkness is, among other things, a historical roman à clef about the internecine wars that dragged on for decades among the Utrians, Humbrians, and Dinutrians—all descended from the same ragtag clutch of peasants and fishermen and kings.

The historical museum in Pakriatz is a timorous affair endowed as an afterthought of a bloated brigand on his deathbed who'd sacked the town all by himself after one drunken carousal in his teens.

hoard
horde

A **hoard** is what has been collected, stored; dragon's gems and gold. It's also the verb that brings such a collection about.

*A*lready obeying their instincts and amassing hoards of trinkets, jewels, tinfoil, copper coins, silverware, and pewter cups, the little dragons kept these caches as well hidden from each other as from the butler, nanny, general factotum—an amazing accomplishment in such a rambunctious setting, but the Schloss was built to house secrets, and obliged even the dimmest of the lot with nooks and crannies, removable stones and floorboards, subterranean passages and crypts.

"It is simply immoral of you to be hoarding all these slips, bustiers, and nighties while many of the boys out on the range have barely a strip of satin to their names," Yolanta added to a reproach that was already calling forth tears of remorse and handkerchiefs of begrudging forgiveness.

> A **horde** is a crowd, sometimes construed as unfriendly, such as the conquering hordes that poured out of Lavukistan and across the Mousserousque plains.

*H*ordes of fans accosted Loona in the back streets of Amplochacha and obscure hamlets of Blegue, sometimes in the most awkward situations—while she was arranging a getaway to Casseglasse-par-Broÿe or defacing her own image in a magazine at the coiffeur's, or halfway through a sleight-of-hand costume change in a roadhouse or opera house powder room.

immured
inured

> To **immure** is to enclose within walls; to shut in, seclude, or confine; to imprison. **Inure**, as a transitive verb, means to accustom to hardship, difficulty, pain: toughen, harden, habituate. As an intransitive verb, it means to come into use; to take or have effect; to become beneficial or advantageous. Also *enure*.

*A*pparently, a young girl was immured in this sepulchre and abandoned to the cruel tricks of time," adduced Alfina over the grisly discovery the dragons had made after many twists and turns in the passage and niches of pleasanter memories and themes.

Inured though she was to the curiosity her presence aroused and the unwanted attention she attracted with her sketchbook vagabondage and switchback monologues, Jonquil couldn't shake off the sense that someone was on her trail even in her sleep.

"I'm afraid, darling, I'm going to have to immure myself in my study till I've arranged a *cave canem* that will secure the fascination of readers inured to Crushed Velvet Press's signature tawdry and titillating dénouements," Nada Seria said, taking leave of Monsieur Plume for a sprint on her PowerBook.

"This spell won't inure straight away, so don't get jumpy. In fact, you must feign indifference to its initiation and outcome, forget it was ever uttered," explained the footman—an amateur magician—to Dariushka during one of their thaumaturgical trysts that was recorded in Dariushka's diary as: "Speak to Trask about peacock blue or Vertigo Forest green upholstery for the barouche box."

imperial
imperious

Imperious once applied to emperors and
similar powerful rulers, and now attaches itself
to others resembling them in manner or
commanding presence: domineering, haughty,
overbearing. In different circumstances, to
express a necessity, it means urgent or impera-
tive. **Imperial** most forthrightly does express the
qualities of power, royalty, and empire.

*W*hen, oh when will you understand that my
most imperious need on this earth is to be
within the sound of your raucous voice, the
reach of your one remaining arm, the sight of
you taking off your uniform and slipping your
battered majesty onto my bearskin rug?" wrote
Milanka in a letter that caught up with Troto at
the Battle of Bluttenbad during the second decade of the war.

The imperial palace was surrounded by a racket
of supplicants seeking amnesty for a handful of
pacifists and travel allowances for banned authors writing in forbidden genres and tongues.

Her imperious bearing can be a bit off-putting,
but she's really just one of the boys after she's
knocked back a couple of whiskies and riddled the

atmosphere with expletives in the dialect of her
forebears.

inside
inside of

Forget the **of**. It serves no purpose: the
relationship is already established.

*I*nside the Pink Antlers Saloon, the barmaid was
hurling pleasantries at Sonia Tweazle Scronx,
who was on her third brandy and fifth recitation
of her tribulations at the Schloss.

"No, put the troglodyte *inside* the box, my little
tempest," said Vole Incubite to his second cousin,
who'd offered to help with the send-off you will
read about under *inveigle*.[†]

The night of Drasko Mustafović's alleged, supposed, so-called abduction from Hotel Artaud
(depending on which quidnunc's[†] hypothesis
you entertained), spirits were summoned from
ethereal realms to his ancestral home. The wind
moaned like a gratified hausfrau, then keened
like an ostracized banshee, while inside the
Schloss lamps flickered, grown men whimpered,
and the panther dived under a rumpled bed and

couldn't be coaxed out with words of endearment or saucers of crème fraîche and champagne. The little dragons were nowhere to be found, not even Pasha Partout, but no one dared in such uncertain conditions to venture underground.

insidious
invidious

Insidious behavior is stealthy and directed toward harmful ends, sometimes through entrapment; treacherous; beguilingly malevolent or harmful.

$\mathcal{T}$he impression it gives is deceptively light. In fact, this comedy of manners takes us on a terrifying tour through the most insidious impulses lurking in the human heart," wrote Frodo Asgard of *Ruffians in Chintz* when it opened in Evrique.

Invidious speech, behavior, or writing tends to rouse ill will, hostility, animosity, resentment, or discrimination.

$\mathcal{L}$ou Garou leafleted the north and east sides of every street with invidious polemics against the premier, while on the doorsteps of houses on the south and west sides she deposited pamphlets ablaze with praise for Gavril Dark and his accomplishments in office thus far.

insuperable
insupportable

Insuperable means impossible to overcome: an insuperable obstacle or fear. **Insupportable** means impossible to tolerate, put up with; intolerable.

$\mathcal{T}$he guide says this face of the mountain is insuperable, but I say let's lasso our caution to a Fata Morgana and tramp on till we plummet.

"This suspense is becoming insupportable!" said Jonquil of a night that showed no sign of ever ending.

intense
intensive

Emotions are **intense**; sustained application or attention is **intensive**. *Intense* arises from within; *intensive* comes from without—that is, it's imposed, assumed.

*M*y feelings for him are intense, but my thoughts are otherwise engaged," explained Jacaranda to her man-eating sidekick, who was giving widowhood such a bad name.

I'm taking a carefree tutorial in thermodynamics and an intensive seminar in Samotrian, a moribund[†] but influential language.

Mafia
Mafioso

"Well, *carí donne,* which word when?" asked Startling Glower of the stiletto-heeled thugs in angora suits on his set the evening they took over "Up Your Eponym" (the title and credits accompanied by obscene Italian gestures) and then stayed on to take over the station and its satellites. They never answered, so I had to look it up myself.

Mafia is for the organization devoted to crime, and can also take a lowercase *m*. A **Mafioso** is an individual member, becoming Mafiosi or Mafiosos when multiplied. We have taken liberties here to feminize the word for a single gangster who is part of the Belladonna mob. Since they have commandeered more than their share of this book, they will appear no further on this page.

*Y*es, the Mafia has become quite a patron of the arts; several of the Mafiosi in Palermo are major backers of some of the most avant-garde composers and kinetic artisans.

masterful
masterly

Sometimes used interchangeably, these two can also become more specific in meaning— **masterful** for dominating, imposing, in command, imperious, **masterly** for showing the skill of a master.

*T*he delivery was masterful, but the message left me completely in the lurch," said one of the cowboys at the Pink Antlers Saloon following a tele-vised address by Queen Maud written especially for the country's cattle rustlers and outlaws and urging fecklessness on the lonesome range.

"Oh! What masterly use you are making of your silences and your predicates tonight!" com-mented Startling Glower during an effervescent lull in the conversation he was taping with Jou-bert Plume and his bride, the tongue-tied Nada Seria, hard at work on *To Die in a Dirndl* and in-tolerant of interruptions.

Ziggie usually got her way through blackmail if her manipulations and masterful tone of voice failed to force the captain's hand. It was through a combination of all three that the *Scarlatina* wound up in ports on no passenger's itinerary where Ziggie was trafficking in bric-a-brac and less innocuous contraband.

may
might

"When does might make right?" asked Zapaduško Ludović of his military mentor shortly after taking his vows of bellicosity and donning his uniform. Oh, reader, this is a conundrum of fearsome contours and staggering surfaces! So much so that I preferred wandering off onto the battlefield before pawing through Fossilblast's notes tucked into a naughty valentine. If you want to express likelihood, **may** is the more optimistic. **Might** in the same sentence diminishes the probability, injects a greater shadow of doubt. That's in the present tense, anyway. But complications upset this neat distinction. **May** also carries the idea of permission, so if you wish to steer clear of that interpretation, as you may in a particular instance, use **might** to suggest likelihood, after all. For instance, in Nada Seria's *Giovanna's Mortgage,* the sentence "She may put her haunted house on the market if it passes the test with our phantom kit" is ambiguous. The real estate agent making this statement could mean that it's likely she will, once the phantom has been authenticated, but perhaps he means that she will be *permitted* to sell the place after the test results are in. To avoid this ambiguity and put across the first meaning, he should have said "She might put her haunted house on the market if it passes the test with our phantom kit." And now we come to the past tense, with its own cases in point! When you want to shift into hindsight, **might** is preferred, even though **may** is not strictly incorrect.

*I*might have lost my key chain in the same place where I must have lost my keys.

Well! You might have given me a ring to tell me you were asleep!

They might have dropped the package off on the wrong doorstep, so our target may still be standing.

"I may have the ultimate answer from the beyond this very evening!" intimates a medium, trying to persuade an equivocating widow to brave a blizzard in her Audi and attend a séance whose numbers are dwindling among the quick if not among the deceased, although the number of the latter might swell if all of the former hit the road.

"To put it quite brutally, sir, we may not be able to find your friend even if he does have a great sense of rhythm," said the American consulate in Rio de Janeiro, which had followed Buenos Aires in the dentist's and robot's sentimental tour of the Southern Hemisphere. "By now, his various limbs and attachments may be turned into sidings and windowsills in the favelas—the hillside shantytowns. You may certainly initiate a search yourself if you think you might recognize individual bolts and springs, nuts and screws, mechanical accoutrements, and, of course, the authentic human teeth you fitted him out with yourself as a professional and affectionate favor."

momentarily
momently

> Drat Siltlow, who these days goes by Drat Outlaw when he's playing the renegade, lines up with the laissez-faire minority, which accepts **momentarily** for "in a moment" besides its inarguable "for a moment" denotation.

*J*onquil shivered momentarily till her metabolism made its pact with the chill of the cavern.

Zoë Platgut excuses herself momentarily from comment on this one: she's sorting out a fracas between the cities of Alsmeer and Lumbachen over the look-alike names of their mittelplatzen.

In fact, the battle has become so heated she expects her absence to be prolonged: far from momentary, that is.

> Startling Glower, on "Up Your Momentary Eponym"—an interlude that replaced the commercial—dismissed that word with a shrug, then devoted thirty seconds to **momently**—rarely used, but when it is, synonymously with "from moment to moment"—although like *momentary* in its more casual use, it can also refer to what's on the verge of happening.

*T*he train, due to depart momently, is still discharging a volley of disoriented passengers.

The promontory grew momently more precarious as his mounting vertigo conquered his apathy.

"The time bomb will go off momentarily, so let's blow this caravansary," said one Belladonna to another at the Palaz of Hoon after they'd read each other's tea leaves and faxed the pastry chef several suggestions for cachinnating his Rush of Cochineal cookies and trolloping his tiramisu.

momentary
momentous

Momentary, as you will comprehend even more fully through the next entry, means fleeting, brief, lasting but a moment. Once that's over, it does have a second meaning: impending, about to occur at any moment.

*P*lease forgive this momentary silence—I'm trying to think my way out of it," said Nada in response to Glower's riposte on "Up Your Eponym."

Her momentary rush into volubility more than made up for the awkward pauses her host and husband had entertained with lacunae[†] from her latest novel and a deconstruction of the Albigensian heresy.

Momentous means charged with significance, highlighted in one's perception, of great or far-reaching consequence.

*I*t's a momentous occasion, so let's break out the Veuve Clicquot!" cried the wizard to Jonquil during their own private leave-taking, after he'd reviewed the precautions her expedition required to bring her back still alive and kicking.

General Ludović had effected many momentous decisions on the battlefield, but none left so deep or incarnadine a mark on his name or history as the carnage of Bluttenbad.

nom de plume
nom de guerre
pseudonym

> **Pseudonym** is the all-purpose word for an assumed name, whatever the reason for its acquisition, however briefly it remains.

*V*andals in pinafores raiding lands to the north and west, Madonnas with mustaches, passports with hand-tinted photos and pseudonyms, kitschy first editions and bogus Bosoxian maps—these are some of the enterprises that keep Blegue afloat when bankrupt bandits and devastation come lapping at its borders.

Nom de plume is a pseudonym with a pen and is used by an author for all or part of his / her literary output. **Nom de guerre**, once meaning a name taken only for battle, in days of chivalry or centuries later in the French army, is now tossed about in a cavalier fashion as a more amusing variant of the more banal **pseudonym**. The plural *s* of *nom de guerre* and *nom de plume* is attached to the *nom*.

When Sonia Tweazle Scronx was feeling frisky, Vargas Scronx would shed the nom de plume of Aelfric Valinthrob and crash into their bedchamber as Bronco Affoloupo, his nom de guerre for such urgent occasions.

Strophe Dulac and Nada Seria are both noms de plume of characters we've met in other wrappings. Nada Seria refuses to reveal her real name since she abandoned Natty Ampersand—and her married name will only confuse you in this particular paragraph. Strophe Dulac is still a hot contender for the Tory Auslander chair under his academic nom de guerre Biffle Wohnengeist (practically a plagiarism of Jonquil Mapp's wohnenskirts, which she used to wear to his meandering lectures).

Poet/designer Slap Ordonato took the nom de plume of Rustle Flèche when he assumed editorship of Eloria's culture and couture review *La Mode and the Mind.*

oblivious

> During a weeklong marathon on prepositions, which was very popular with immigrants desperate to set their verbs in the right directions as well as those who blithely translate verb/preposition pairs from their own native languages, Startling Glower allowed that **oblivious** could be followed by either *of* or *to,* as it was then improvised upon by several guests while the others faked semi-consciousness to pantomime the word's connotation.

I'm not oblivious to her attractions, but I prefer boys with taffy in their hair and opals on their toes and fingers," countered Samson to a discreet suggestion posed by the trouble-rustling Yolanta.

"You've been oblivious of others' existence since you misplaced your child in the Quisisana Arcade," said Valeska Tutulescu to her sister, who was nearly catatonic with bereavement.

off
off of

"No no no," abjured Despina, "**of** is extra-marital—I mean extraneous!" So proceeded the little dragons' grammar lesson, with Despina forced into the role of substitute after they'd abandoned their tutor in the linguistic labyrinth to her fate in an oubliette.

*I*f you stray off the trail," read the faux guidebook, "your footprints will disappear along with your memory, and you'll be lost among the shadows of men and beasts from long ago."

"Take these handcuffs off my wrists—and that credenza off my chest!" yawped Flip, thrashing about on the barroom floor in a pool of viscous words.

ominous
onerous

Ominous is boding ill, bearing evil omens, menacing, threatening. **Onerous** is oppressive, burdensome, troublesome, demanding unwilling input.

*T*he onerous task of reassembling the robot was, in fact, a labor of true love for the dentist, who'd tracked down nearly every piece essential to their resumption of fox-trots beneath the stars and dance hall marathons.

"That's an ominous undertone, and I don't care for the overt message, either," said Jonquil, listening to a threat on her answering machine about laying off or winding up in an ossuary.

Ominous signs loomed dark on the horizon and dragged off the evening with them.

oscillate
osculate

To **oscillate** is to swing back and forth with a steady, uninterrupted rhythm; to waver. To **osculate** is to kiss!

*J*acaranda, a fresh-air fiend, installed herself in a desultory compartment of the train, pulled off her stockings (under the latest edition of *Der zaftig Tagblut*), rotated her head gracefully, propped her feet on the knees of the passenger snoring opposite her, and broke out the oscillating fan she'd last used during one of Beau Romano's incandescent tantrums.

"Now really, is it strictly verboten to chat and osculate awhile?" parried the baba, batting her eyelashes, as the Grim Reaper advanced with his open cloak and his rusty, impetuous scythe.

outside
outside of

Outside need not be followed by this tagalong, supernumerary preposition.

I shall remain outside the realm of death for as long as I find you amusing," she continued, rummaging about for the angostura bitters and tossing him her bridal bouquet with a well-aimed dart of flattery.

Outside the town of Pakriatz a placid storm lay biding its time and gathering its fearsome voices.

"We have no other information about Flak Gravitas outside the profile with which you've been provided," dissimulated Serafima's anonymous employers when he pressed them, via a post office box in a village near Alsmeer, for further details on the object of his espionage.

practical
practicable

Practicable means feasible (an operation, plan, design) or usable for a specified purpose. The Whore of Babel adds that however much use you make of your friends or enemies, you could never call them *practicable*: the human race takes exception to this adjective. **Practical** can describe a sensible, efficient person—one gifted for putting ideas or things into practice or discerning their real potential. A promiscuous word, it enjoys a handful of other applications.

*T*his is the practical part of the book; the lexicon is embroidery, the frosting on the cake.

"Is this really a practicable instrument for charming the pants off the provincials?" asked the harpist, who was taking his leave of Duchess Ilona with much regret and hesitation.

Jacaranda found her silk stockings (a present from an admirer she'd met at a *boulangerie* while under the influence of cocoa laced with the local poppy seeds) most practical for tying up banditti who attempted to waylay her during untrammeled shopping sprees.

"But you're practically the only person who knows the other side of me!" yipped Rip in the midst of a brutal rejection.

Jonquil's practical grasp of geography was elevated by a searing sense of mystery that led her onto trails of ill repute and through mountains of minatory[†] majesty.

"A full-scale career and sanguinary smorgasbord will not be practicable with his bite as it is," explained the dentist to Dodeska Tutulescu as they stared into her son's open maw. "You'll need an additional visit with the technician who will be crafting the crowns that will lengthen and sharpen the points of these teeth—and once you've seen him, we'll take it from there, over another six weeks and fifty-five thousand zlotky."

"Where, oh where shall I get the money?" wailed Dodeska, a practical woman who'd even had a go at her son's jugular to encourage the extrusion of his fangs.

precipitate
precipitous

> **Precipitate** means moving rapidly, recklessly;
> impulsive, hasty, as in the precipitate decision
> Nada Seria made to switch publishers (from
> Crushed Velvet Press to the House of Ama-
> ranth) with her tropical novella *Taxi to the Other
> Island*, when Bluestocking Press was waiting
> just around the corner with a much more
> interesting offer: either she change genres, or
> they'd mug her. **Precipitous** is more physically
> dangerous, even terror-strickening, since it
> belongs to a precipice: a precipitous path,
> ledge, road, from any of which one might
> carelessly plunge to one's death.

I mean, I find your modus operandi entirely too precipitate. I expected an almost imperceptible shadow creeping about with stealth and discretion, giving me time to fetch my gloves and handbag, polish my glasses and powder my nose, not this bullfight with a total stranger in the middle of my rumpled parlor in stark, dazing daylight!" continued the baba, brandishing the fire tongs at her guest, who had neither rung nor rapped the brass knocker but materialized out of her television screen during a video of *Truly, Madly, Deeply.*

"The pass is precipitous on a clement day, fatal when the heavens are raging," warned the faux guidebook that had been concocted to protect endangered and endangering vistas.

predominate
predominant
preponderate

> **Predominate** is the verb, although it masquerades as an adjective under the auspices of Webster. If you want a genuine adjective to play with, with a gang of authority backing you, take **predominant**. **Preponderate** can mean *predominate*, but its narrower, original definition carries weight: to be heavier. More broadly, it means to be superior in strength, power, influence, number: to *predominate*.

What predominates in the most popular songs of contemporary Lavukistan is a sense of having gone astray, of shifting borders, of bewilderment bordering on bedlam and a dread of what tomorrow might spirit away.

"The predominant mood at Count Ghastly's house these days is a triple-layered wanhope frosted with a fitful gloom," explained the village pastry chef to a tea shop of quidnuncs[†] and gossips whose schadenfreude was snapping up crumbs of rueful news.

Testimony on behalf of Frotteau Dessange preponderated at the pub, but a fat lot of good that did him when he appeared in court!

premier
premiere

Premier is the head of state or cabinet in countries that have one and don't call him/her prime minister. These include France and its former foreign colonies. It's also the title in Canada and Australia for the heads of provincial governments. As an adjective, *premier* means first in rank, chief, or first in time, earliest, oldest. A **premiere** is the opening night of any spectacle: movie, musical, opera, theatrical production. Like *debut,* it has gradually taken on the trappings of a verb and become promiscuous, applying not only to the world or national premiere of a given work, but to its opening night in town. What's more, it can hop media, so that a movie can premiere on television long after it's disappeared from the big screen.

*I*n a blazing, blind rush for the fire exits, the audience at the premiere of Clackengirth's opera trampled the minister of culture, critic Cedric Moltgang, five French poodles (part of the cast), the minister of public safety, and the dashing young premier, Gavril Dark,* whose hand still clutched a beaded ceinture from Mog Cinders' prêt-à-partir flight gown, a creation of Gregor Schlaffenfuss.

"This supercilious piece of scholarship on the Maloropians is absolutely first-class, premier, top drawer, cat's meow," said Jonquil's last, lone advocate in the department before her total fall from grace.

Savage Nocturne premiered at Pakriatz's pleasure dome to a full house of connivers and banditti.

* son of the eminent solicitor

prescribe
proscribe

> In its general sense, **prescribe** means to set
> down as a rule or guide; in its medical sense, to
> recommend so legally that a pharmacist will
> comply. **Proscribe** means to denounce, con-
> demn; to forbid, prohibit.

*F*or situations where sulking, seduction, and
subterfuge threatened to be bootless, the Belladonna Mafia prescribed brazen hussiness to
clinch a coveted deal.

In Act I, Scene VII of *Adipose Rex* the cardiologist
proscribes suckling pig, crème fraîche, lobster,
and pastitsio, while the protagonist weeps, his
chins and belly aquiver, into a platter of pralines
and profiteroles.

It was too late to prescribe anything for Pasha
Partout: his nature was having its way.

pretense
pretext

A **pretext** has more slyness mixed into its
falsity: it's a misleading action or statement of
purpose, deliberately concealing the true
motive, which may be dishonest in yet another
way. **Pretense** is the act of pretending, a fabric
of make-believe, and when it metamorphoses
into a related noun, *pretension* (often occurring
as plural), it means affectation.

*U*nder the pretext of slipping out for a smoke, Rip
made off for his assignation in the back of a big
blue truck.

"The didactic pretext of these books has become
quite a lucrative subterfuge and a deadly serious
art," confessed or dissimulated Cram Fossilblast
in his infamous "Whore of Babel" interview with
Rafael Todos los Muertos.

"This pretense that you don't really mean what
you say is a kamikaze cop-out," countered Rafael,
hoping to provoke further indiscretions and up
the magazine's pretentious readership.

The Gallimaufs have always been above cheap pretensions: even their address is an understatement that puts homeless girls at ease and fills desperadoes with disdain.

principal
principle

> Of these two, only **principal** can play the gadabout role of an adjective, one meaning most important, main, first, highest, foremost. As a noun, it takes either human or monetary form: an amount of money or a person top in rank, first in authority.

*T*he Mousserousque is the principal river in the luscious valley of that name.

The principal contenders for the Tory Auslander chair started parlaying the basest of tactics as the competition entered its final weeks.

"The principal will be due at the end of the year, unless you care to parcel out your soul within a much more generous time frame, since we're talking Eternity here," said one of the arch fiends tempting the trammeled protagonist of *Giovanna's Mortgage*.

"We'll see what the principal has to say about this!" said Beau Romano's kindergarten teacher, playing her pathetic trump card much too early in the game.

Principle is strictly a noun meaning rule, law, motivating force, fundamental truth.

*N*ot all the rivers of Azuriko obey the fluvial principle of making for the sea.

"My God, man, have you no principles left to honor or betray?" Nimbo asked Trill Apasaguena, who was looking more like a monster than a mogul in the Mitteleuropean economy.

purposefully
purposely

Purposefully describes actions and demeanor
that exhibit a strong intention, that express
determination, goal-orientation. **Purposely**
means intentionally, deliberately, and could be
used in the same contexts as *on purpose*.

*C*ertain that Beau Romano was responsible for the
mishap on the moat, Jacaranda strode purposefully into the dragons' playroom to smack the little devil in his chops and hang him by his tail till
dusk. Saskiak,* though, trundled forth as a wit-
ness, crying, "But he didn't do it purposely!" and
Sonia Tweazle Scronx, besotted with Beau Romano since his babyhood, backed up this out-
burst of solidarity, however gravely she doubted
its truth.

* the dragon also known as Little Boy Blue for the
cobalt flames he snorted

rain
reign
rein

Reign means to rule, as a king or queen, or hold sway as just about anything with such impressive power—often elemental forces or emotions. It is sometimes misused in the expression **to rein in**, such as Yolanta would do with her mustang or Amaranthia with her predatory concupiscence. **Rain** falls from the heavens, and blessings can rain upon you, your mate, your fate, estate.

*R*ain and snow are responsible for only part of Azuriko's wanton waterscapes. Springs appear overnight throughout the land, as mysteriously as truffles, in remote regions and close to town, even bursting through city cobblestones with a might you'd never guess lay murmuring in these god-given, plangent fountains. One passage of the Twenty-Third Psalm has been abridged according to local conditions—where it reads "He maketh me to lie down in still waters"—since this is incomprehensible to many congregations.

"Whoa there!" said Dante, reining in his palomino with greater conviction than he was reining in his runaway crush on the elusive Dusty Saxon.

Darkness reigned for forty days and nights, and nefarious creatures and malefic intentions wantoned about the towns in white nightgowns and crept into the water supply, cinemas, tram cars, and intercoms till life was suffused with their ethos.

> As a noun, **reign** is the period during which a particular monarch is wearing the crown. It also applies to his/her authority, sovereignty.

*D*uring the reign of Incognito V, improvements revealed the monarch's proclivities in no uncertain terms: bicycle paths commandeered the most scenic routes, rerouting coaches and carriages to marshlands, abysses, fens, crevasses, and panoramas of agrarian monotony in his own and other countries.

It rained blood day and night for a week in Cendrac, then the precipitation ran clear and cool and clean as if to wash the shocking sight away. "Are we washed in the blood of the lamb, or is this slaughterhouse landscape a visitation of the massacres perpetrated by our soldiers?" one editorial posed to the province's citizens, who would be deluged with more of such chastenings.

"Rein in your desperadoes, or I'll wrap them all in lace!" read the telegram from Queen Maud to the three monarchs of Trajikistan.

rebound
redound

It takes resilience (or a desire to get even) to **rebound**, which means to spring back; as a noun, it conveys a bounce, one that comes in response: a bouncing-back. **Redound** means to add to, contribute, to have an effect or a result.

*O*n the rebound from his nasty breakup with a cunning, unflappable† cartographer, Torquil hopped a freighter headed for the Odessa Steps via Patagonia.

"Your tumultuous good looks and polished phrases will redound to the mistrust your position and family history inspire in subjects both benighted and enlightened," Incognito VI warned his eldest son, about to succeed the dying monarch.

I can't say I'm exactly rebounding from these smutty allegations, but my advisers, wife, and mistresses are stanching the flow of information and barking up my every assertion.

rebuff

A **rebuff** is often imbued with scorn, contempt and usually involves rejecting a person, not a thing (suggestion, proposal, document, tank rolling through your beloved metropolis with malicious intentions).

*D*o you mean to say you're rebuffing me?" asked Torquil, reeling from Jonquil's awkward announcement in the Amplochacha cathedral.

In *Giovanna's Mortgage* (Nada Seria's novel of romance and real estate), the heroine wrestles to the ground a tricky dilemma: whether to stay with her boyfriend, a consummate creep who does the housework under general anesthetic, or move in with a certified phantom. In a spine-tingling dénouement, she rebuffs the domestic mesomorph and embraces a restless spirit determined to master the amatory arts before shuffling off to an assignation in Eternity with an amateur alchemist (a married woman of lofty position in her mortal life and of curious, mottled mien in the sweet hereafter).

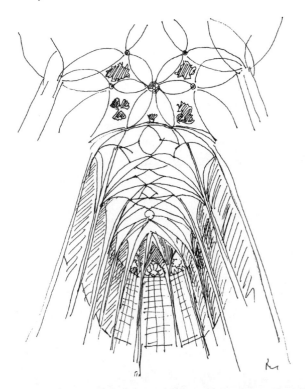

repel
repulse

Repel means to resist, to ward off, reject, fight against, and also to fill with disgust or distaste, to provoke aversion. **Repulse** can be used in the same ways (except according to the most fastidious usage mongers, who withhold the latter sense of the word while conceding that the adjective *repulsive* is at the heart of the confusion in the overlap), but its more precise meaning is to drive away, to spurn, to reject brusquely, coldly.

*W*hen Kristiana's about, the panther can't be counted on to repulse unwanted visitors, spies, and robbers from the Schloss, so Drasko Mustafović has had to install an elaborate security system that causes more grief to the butler, nanny, general factotum, and Jacaranda than banditti dropping in for antisocial calls with the Grim Reaper in tow," explained Ilona to her lover as a false alarm once again resounded through the halls and Saskiak and Beau Romano scuttled out of sight to dissolve in scampish shrieks of laughter over the rampant panic they'd set in motion with a well-aimed flick of their tails.

"It is true I did nothing to repel his advances," wrote Katya in her diary before Hotel Artaud had become a habit, "nor did he make the slightest move or squeak to discourage my outright attraction."

"I find his baby-faced ghoulishness repelling yet complaisant," wrote Rip in his diary of a new acquaintance he'd struck with a match and an English cigarette that night at Blotto Junction.

Repulsed far too briskly in the second skirmish, the Azurikoan army sadly disgraced its picturesque scenery and its impractical countrymen.

respectfully
respectively

Respectfully is an adverb of attitude—full of respect, in a respectful manner—and takes its place repeatedly as an acceptably neutral sign-off to an impersonal letter.

*K*atya curtsied respectfully when visiting dignitaries were shown through the Schloss but took great liberties in following her whims as soon as she was out of the sight of the strictest disciplinarians.

Sorely vexed and yet respectfully yours,
Pablito Crusodopolis

> **Respectively** calls attention to a specified order, arranges things in time and space.

*C*atastrophe, cacophony, and monotony set the tone during the reigns of, respectively, Incognito VIII, Prolix XI, and Maud.

I've placed my bets in the last three races on Marco Polo, Northern Lights, and Meet Me on the Other Side of Beauty, respectively.

senseless
insensible

> **Senseless** means having taken leave of one's
> senses in any of several ways: by losing con-
> sciousness, succumbing to a lapsus; by going
> mad or appearing so through doing something
> foolish, i.e., showing a lack of common sense
> or reason; by being dim in comprehension and
> perception. **Insensible** can describe similar
> inattention, unconsciousness, but also applies
> to a lack of emotion, responsiveness, sensa-
> tion, appreciation, awareness of any stimulus
> or fellow creature.

$\mathcal{T}$hat credenza coulda knocked me senseless!"
bawled Flip, crawling anfractuously to the saloon door for a double shot of prairie air and a
possible getaway car.

We'll have no more of these senseless inferences,
O.K., honey? I've never seen Trajikistan, let alone
this Inn of the Sixth Unhappiness—so unless my
credit card checked in and had breakfast on the
balcony without me, it must be a mix-up with the
numbers.

"I am not insensible to your trials and tribulations—it can't be easy keeping all these formulas
straight—but I really fear you dealt my minotaur

a deadly philtre," said the grief-stricken proprietor of Hotel Artaud to the sorceress who ran the apothecary.

Ziggie prided herself on being insensible to gossip and violent temperature changes, so when she found herself inordinately affected, she had to fake the *désinvolture* for which she was both admired and reviled.

sinecure
cynosure

A **cynosure** is a person or thing or phenomenon attracting attention or admiration by its brilliance, éclat, aura, or interest; a center of attention or source of guidance, inspiration, or direction. A **sinecure** is a position or office providing honor or profit but requiring little or no work, a cushy arrangement indeed.

*L*ong a cynosure in the world of opera and fashion, Constanza Zermattress liked to occasionally let down her sable hair and go slumming in the hinterlands with lounge lizards, defrocked priests, and suburban cowboys.

Offered a lucrative sinecure for keeping his mouth shut, the attaché shredded his shorthand and took an axe to his laptop (an accessory to crime and high treason).

stalactite
stalagmite

> You enter a cavern and are confronted with pointed protrusions coming out of the ceiling and floor. The ones overhead are **stalactites**. The ones underfoot are **stalagmites**.

*A*ghast and agoggle at the stalactites over their makeshift bed (two parkas, one poncho, an ancient map of their approximate trek), Jonquil and Drasko Mustafović, Jr., lightened the darkness with ardent alacrity and a sudden state of undress.

The banditti, under hot pursuit and in hounded distress, hurled themselves into a cavern and gouged their feet (some wore moccasins, some wore sandals, four had lost their shoes altogether while flitting through a mirage) on a carpet of stalagmites, their howls harmonizing in awkward intervals with the squeaks of motherless bats.

stanch
staunch

Although these two are related and can go either way, each has its preference for what it should convey in a sentence: **stanch** as a verb meaning to stop a flow, **staunch** as an adjective meaning steady, firm, loyal, steadfast, and when applied to vessels, watertight.

*T*he *Scarlatina* was staunch last time they'd checked, but of a sudden, in the Bay of Oublanskaia, it started to sink, and the more nimble passengers wound up on life rafts with a delegation of Danutrian rats bound for a confab in Constantinople.

Staunch friends already by the age of nine, the little vampires swore eternal brotherhood as they mixed their blood from fresh incisions, then stanched each other's wounds with red silk handkerchiefs their mothers bought by the monogrammed, deluxe dozen.

Can no one stanch the flow of our most precious goods and resources down the waterways of Azuriko while nothing comes to us in return but a spate of suspicious characters?

stationary
stationery

> Something that's **stationary** doesn't move; it
> sticks to its station. **Stationery** contains the
> ending of the word *paper*, of which it is made.

*N*othing in our universe is stationary or pre-
dictable. Even God is a scamp who likes to de-
camp and send out the sure-fire signals of a
polymorph in agitation," blasphemed Strophe
Dulac as a preface to her deconstruction of *Out
of the Loud Hound of Darkness.*

The clue that clapped investigators' suspicions on
Frotteau Dessange was a note found on the Inn of
Serenity and Iniquity stationery apostrophizing a
shoeshine girl in the Quisisana Arcade who had
handled his alligator boots with the touch of a
killer temptress.

sympathy
empathy

Empathy involves a vicarious participation in another's suffering, identifying with someone else's problems through imagination or having had a similar experience. This gemütlich abstract noun has sired two synonymous adjectives: *empathic* and *empathetic*. **Sympathy** doesn't come quite so close, however much compassion or pity for another's troubles it conveys, however much understanding and sharing are felt or proclaimed. *Sympathy* has a wider embrace, too, applying not only to pain: *sympathy* also conveys congeniality, shared interests, affability, the sense of kinship that *affinity* implies. Thus *sympathetic* might be tossed about at Blotto Junction in response to a patted shoulder, offered handkerchief, or else through a surge of sudden, hopeful friendship as two strangers air their views, relate their life stories, strip down to their first names: "I find you very sympathetic."

A wave of empathy swept through the Doppelgäng when they heard of the humiliating roundup of a band of their brigand brethren.

"We are nothing if not empathic," avouched the chorus of *The Velveteen Rabble* shortly before the conflagration.

"Can I offer you a tumbler of tea or a cup of sympathy?" asked a smarmy waitress in a leather suit at a tea shop known to Lumbacheners and out-of-towners for its gemütlichkeit.

Beloved King Alabastro, oh monarch of aching hearts!

In sending you my condolences, I cannot claim to offer you unmitigated empathy, because of course your wife and your bereavement are exquisitely unique—but I do share with you a degree of attachment, that is, to my husband's raiments and accessories, tokens of his presence I find impossible to relinquish: a half-smoked Gauloise cigarette in an ashtray we stole from our hotel room at Lake Bled; his tuxedo, which I don occasionally when expecting unwelcome guests; the sheet music on the piano, open to "Mein Blut ist dein Frühstück," the last song he ever played; and his reading glasses, which still gleam at me from our bedside table and interpret my hypnagogic imagery and the footnotes to my dreams.

With deepest sympathy,
Amanda Trust

tight
tightly

Startling Glower grappled with this pair of querulous twins on a program called "Shut Your Face," a command he proceeded to obey: the subject seemed to render him speechless for the first seven minutes, unless he was simply demonstrating a jaw clenched tight, or a tightly sealed pair of lips. When he finally opened up, he explained that the choice depends on whether it's the result or the application of the process (of shutting, closing, freezing, clamping) that calls for emphasis. If you want to focus on a state that endures for quite some time once it's been achieved (by freezing, shutting, etc.), **tight** is your word, indeed.

*H*olding the reins tightly, Dante Kaputo let his thoughts gallop ahead while his horse had an apoplectic seizure.

Miranda shut her eyes tight and fluttered her nostrils in a beguiling semblance of somnolence so the sandman would beat it and leave her to the latest novelette by Nada Seria.

"Hold me tight, baby, and don't let go until I stop this shivering," said Jesperanda, who had had a shock at Chichikov & Company and was determined to make the most of it.

A few more finesses are in order:

Tight can only *follow* the verb. If you want tightness to precede it, it has to go by **tightly**. *Tight* is also a component of several idiomatic expressions in which *tightly* would never do: *sleep tight* and *sit tight*.

*T*he gates and doors to the Villa Lugubria were tightly shut, but the curtains had been riven† by Count Ghastly's hounds, so much could be discerned through the brambles and windows with a pair of sharp eyes or binoculars.

Sleep tight, my precious, and when you wake tomorrow, all these ruffians will be history.

"Sit tight, you little monsters, and let me read the end of the story—or don't you want to know how Saint George slew the dragon?" said Sonia as her charges fidgeted and stuck gumdrops in Pasha Partout's nose and ears and tickled him with the flamingo feathers Jonquil had trailed through the hallways and breakfast room.

tousle
tussle

A **tousle** is a rumpled, disheveled mass of whatever you can suggest into such a shape; to **tousle** is to dishevel, rumple, or disarray. To **tussle** is to scuffle, put up a rough struggle— which is what it means as a noun.

*O*dious was always game for a tussle, especially if it involved a bit of cat-and-mouse followed by flying fur.

Kristiana sleepwalked into the Schloss's most sumptuous *salle de bain,* where two cowboys were enjoying a midnight session of sybaritics, and startled them into a state of consternation with her tousled mane and full-speed, unfaltering advance.

Once they'd redirected her steps down the hall toward Amaranthia's chambers, their delicious languor had been so thoroughly disrupted that they tussled themselves into a rampageous state and sacked the bedroom occupied by a judge from Evrique before continuing with their ablutions and aqueous sprawl, their towels in a tousle in the corner.

vanish
vanquish

> To **vanish** is to disappear. To **vanquish** is to soundly beat or conquer, to subdue in a battle, conflict, showdown—military or metaphorical.

*E*ach night Jonquil would sketch maps of the territory she had discovered that day, and on awakening she would discover that the lines, lakes, villages, and mountain ranges had vanished without a trace.

"Well, we didn't exactly vanquish the enemy," reported General Ludović from his customary table at Café Sans Souci, "but we flummoxed them with a few etymological and ontological questions."

Having vanquished her fears for the night through prayers to the goddess of mercy (she had already vanquished her scruples about abusing bedtime visitors), Miranda summoned the sandman from under the bed, where she'd left him gagged and bound the previous evening while she drifted dreamily through the dénouement of *The Bad-Tempered Cavalier.*

virtuousness
virtuosity

Virtuousness is the presence or abundance of virtue; **virtuosity** is a stunningly proficient level and habit of performance.

$\mathcal{P}$rolix XI will be remembered not for his winning way with vagrant ruffians or his wanton displays of virtuousness, but for the tacky monuments he commissioned and the wrack and ruin of his realm.

"What beguiled me about Primo Talentito besides his virtuosity on the oboe was his clipped and crisp delivery of both compliments and reprehensions," wrote Constanza in an abbreviated account of her infatuation with the maestro from Mirudana.

whence

It's not ever "from whence." The *from* is contained in **whence**.

*C*endrac, the province whence we come, is rarely rinsed by rain, and our rivers run black with blood.

A *Cave Canem*
Companion
Lexicon

abjure

to repudiate or retract, especially with formal
solemnity; to recant; to renounce, forswear

I can abjure infinity with equanimity, my wolf cub
with reluctance, and August at Lake Sandali with
pleasure, but never, never shall I renounce my
bat-wing breastplate, tricorne of rabbit fur, and
the felt slippers I padded off in from that quaint
museum in Pakriatz," said Loona as her agent
threatened her with both abandonment and a
session of discipline.

accoutrement
accouterment

personal clothing, accessories, ancillary
equipment; the outfittings of a soldier besides
dress and weaponry; in plural form, also
trappings

A re these accoutrements really necessary?"
asked Jonquil as she strapped on her snowshoes
and buttoned her bullet-proof bloomers and vest
for their first night in the wilds of upper Lavukistan.

"What a charming bouquet of accouterments!" exclaimed Dodeska Tutulescu as the Swiss army knife unfolded before her eyes, having cut its way through the satin ribbon and crackling paper.

acolyte

an altar assistant in public worship; any assistant, attendant, follower

*G*reat consternation in the cathedral today!" read the *Passevitza Clarion,* which went on to relate the tragedy of a golden, green-eyed acolyte abducted right off the altar by a blob of great chiaroscuro charm that had descended from the choir.

"A table for one, with six acolytes in attendance," said Loona to the maître d'hôtel, tossing her head at the polyglot procession clinging to her petticoats, treading on her heels, hanging on to her every word in a daze of adoring incomprehension.

amorphous

shapeless, lacking definite form or type,
anomalous

*T*he prime suspect—this blob in the Passevitza
cathedral—could you describe it more precisely,
apart from the light and shadow, or was it simply
writhing about as an amorphous mass, with no
one shape holding on for long in its curious yet
purposeful motion? And as it engulfed the altar
boy, was his form discernible, however briefly, in
its contours? Is there any connection between
this ethereal malfeasant and the Velveteen Rabble?" Rafael Todos los Muertos was asking one of
the witnesses of the event that had strengthened
most of the parishioners' faith.

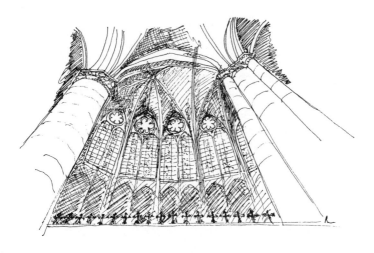

amulet

An **amulet** is a charm that bestows protection: it's worn to ward off evil.

*P*romise me you'll wear this amulet every moment you are out of my sight," the wizard said to Jonquil, about whose safety he was having doubts, considering the texture and remorseless history of the terrain where destiny was demanding her presence.

animadversion

a critical, cutting remark, unfavorable, censorious comment; the act of criticizing

*I*nured to sanctimonious moral judgments from the age of ten, Mog braved this fresh onslaught of animadversions with skittish composure and a giveaway ripple that traveled the length of her celebrated *ensellure.*

anomie

social instability through erosion of values;
alienation and sense of purposelessness of an
individual or social class through such erosion
and dissipation

*A*nomie was the most pernicious legacy of a
century and a half of Samotrian imperialism.

apogee

highest or most exalted point: climax

*I*t's either the apogee of design for this apoplectic decade or a blunder of vast dimensions,"
equivocated Jacomino Vervazzo, withholding his
weighty imprimatur from Eloria's new opera
house—where dislocated divas and truculent
tenors alike declared they would never air their
arias.

appall

to fill with or cause dismay; to fill or overcome
with horror, consternation, or fear; to dismay;
literally, to cause to grow pale, to make pale

"We are aggrieved, contrite, and appalled," began Queen Maud's address to her subjects when laundered news of the Bluttenbad rout first broke through official ranks.

"I'll take only so much of this appalling behavior," bluffed Jacaranda as the little dragons continued work on the beaded frock in which they intended to enmesh her.

atavistic

An **atavistic** trait or characteristic is one that reappears after several generations; **atavistic** behavior or patterns recur after a period of absence or abeyance.

*T*hose topaz eyes are atavistic," Katya was explaining to Jacaranda in defense of her cousin's weird mien and sudden disappearances. "My great-great-grandmother's sister, who married a banker in Budapest, was said to have held the bishop of Alsmeer in thrall with irises that very color."

"Must be something atavistic," muttered the vet, prodding the comatose creature with his tongs, testing its reflexes with a mallet, wafting charred flesh and melted chocolate past its snout, and otherwise trying to rouse it.

attrition

a rubbing down, wearing away by friction; a
gradual diminution in number or strength
because of constant stress

*Y*ou *know* I don't like being catty," said Boris
Marcelovsky in reply to an impertinent question
about the Duchess Ilona, "but—how shall I put
it? She's not exactly ravaged . . . perhaps what I
see in her eyes, her décolletage, and along the
curves of her shoulders is a trace of attrition
since the last time she consecrated her tousle of
hair to my hands."

"We'll whop their asses with demagoguery and attrition, then finish them off with my grandma's
musket," purred General Ludović as he studied
the advancing armies through his auntie's opera
glasses.

belletristic

> This is the adjective you wind up with when you want to put across the realm and qualities of belles lettres: literature with aesthetics at its heart, not information or polemics; writing, often on literature and aesthetics, that is distinguished by its style.

The Loneliness of the Bluestockinged Mugger is about a belletristic soi-disant prima donna who takes her salon so seriously that none of the bright stars of arts and letters can bear to shine in her presence.

"Well! Wasn't that a belletristic apéritif," said Flip, sliding off the barstool after five Campari and sodas and a harangue by Yolanta about the symbolism of lace on boxer shorts in the myths of Mitteleuropa.

carte blanche

unconditional authority, full discretionary
power

*I*f you feel tempted to abuse this carte blanche
you've been handed, please dial that emergency
number we've tattooed on your wrist and carved
into the top of your desk," urged the cabinet
members Gavril Dark had inherited from his
wounded predecessor, who continued to call the
shots from his bed.

"Does this carte blanche include sexual favors?"
wondered the new minister of money and war as
the valet in whose hands he now found himself
combed the tassels of his epaulettes and adjusted
the ramrod on its cerebrospinal path.

casuistry

clever but false reasoning; act or process
of settling questions of right and wrong in
conduct

*C*ountering the countess's assertions with calibanter and casuistries, Nemo was reserving a Gordian knot in the Procrustean bedsheets for his contretemps with the queen.

caveat

a warning or caution

*C*ave canem is but one of many caveats giving visitors and peddlers pause at the entrance of Count Ghastly's mournful estate, which has become known to the polysyllabics in the neighborhood as the Villa Lugubria.

cave canem

Beware of the dog.

cerements
cerement cloth

burial garment

*T*ake off those cerements, baby, and pour me a café au lait," is one of the lines of "We Had a Continental Breakfast Kind of Love" that betrays its author's morbid state of mind.

circumlocution

use of language that skirts around one's meaning (if indeed one has a meaning) with excessive wordiness (or prolixity), hence indirect, evasive speech or writing; a round-about expression

*W*hen Startling Glower introduced a game called Circumlocutions to his "Up Your Eponym" audience, the inventions were so richly ridiculous that this verbal frolic continues on an occasional basis (it requires a certain focused inattention of the guests), and indeed *these* pages have been inspired and visited by its loopy, grandiloquent inventions.

By the seventh day of their battle of wits, the baba was asizzle with her own brilliance, and the Grim Reaper was feeling dizzy from both his personal centrifugal force and his antagonist's circumlocutions.

clinquant

glittering with gold or tinsel

*A*s you will see in *Benighted Kingdoms,* there is a clinquant quality to all these countries that complements the darkness.

columbarium

a sepulchral vault with niches and recesses to receive the ashes of the dead, or any such recess

*C*ount Ghastly would often promenade his sorrows through the chambers of the columbarium, mumbling to himself the names of inhabitants interspersed with bits of Dante, Milton, *De Profundis,* and pages from the bootlegged diary of Capriccio.

confabulate

> To **confabulate** is to converse informally or
> privately. *Confab* is a casual form of such a
> conversation: a *confabulation*. In psychiatry
> **confabulate** means to fill a gap in memory with
> a falsification believed to be true.

*L*ook, we don't have time to wrestle with these
ontological questions or confabulate about the
lupine beast lurking in your closet—the ship is
definitely going under, and I'm not going with it.

"Allow me, my dear, to confabulate here a moment," said Jonquil's professor of ethics over the pages of her term paper and a fatal cappuccino. "Did these delectable kneecaps of yours never stir improper thoughts in the minds of your four brothers or the evangelist who lived two doors down with his goat named Satyr?"

And what was the upshot of these confabulations over several shots of slivovitz and a map with clinquant borders? A journey that would take twenty years to start and still no time in the planning.

congeries

a collection or aggregation

The parliament of Azuriko is usually a congeries of scattered and fragile pavilions which handsomely supports many strapping youths and architects through its frequent devastations.

craven

cowardly; contemptibly timid

*K*ing Placido IV (better known as Placido the Craven) had allowed a narcoleptic horde of white-gloved barbarians to shuffle into Louvelandia with their housecats and cushions and camera obscura, throw down their mattresses in the midst of Maloropia, and between naps beget a generation of ferocious—*

> * With regrets, we must print this sentence unfinished: it was written by a descendant of those very barbarians under an atavistic spell of somnolence.

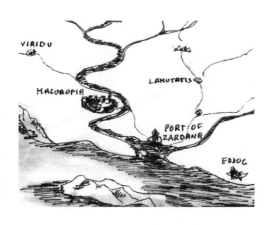

cretaceous

resembling or containing chalk

*T*he effect of this new foundation is positively cre-
taceous!" gloated one vampire to another as they
applied a midnight pallor over their roseaceous,
macho good looks.

cursory

going rapidly over something without noticing
details; hasty; superficial

A cursory glance after they'd done their mouths
and eyes assured them both that their sockets
seemed cadaverous, their irises incandescent,
their lips luscious with desire. On closer inspec-
tion, however, they decided to tweeze their eyebrows into arresting art deco angles and dust
their cheekbones with Cyanosis No. 9.

dearth

a scarcity, lack, shortage

A dearth of mirth is what we expected of Trajik-istan—not this welter of follies and festivators.

debouch

> to march out (as from a defile) into open
> ground; to pass out; to emerge

*P*ast Le Lac aux Cendres debouches a vertiginous trail through a tempest of trees to the Torrents of Tremblovatz.

The soldiers under General Pvbxtrz's command debouched in a malformation of mass disorder onto the Meadow of Muted Nightingales by the River Mousserousque.

demotic

popular; vulgar

*N*ever regard the demotic will with indifference or scorn," croaked Incognito VI to his son (still athrill with wet dreams and fast cars) as his deathbed counsel droned on. "With satellite television, the Internet, and virtual reality, the vox populi* has become a force inconceivable in my own youth—so show discretion and justice in your public persona, at least, and circumspection in your dealings with thugs."

demurral

a restrained, polite, mild, coy, or considered expression of opposition; the act of demurring, or objecting

*D*espina's demurral (she was showing an absolute aversion to leadership of late) left Alfina as the head of the expedition into a secret passageway Pasha Partout had awakened in during a somnambulistic stroll with his pince-nez propped over his snout and his pajamas tied to his throat.

* the voice of the people; popular opinion

deracinate

to uproot; to displace from one's native habitat
or accustomed environment

*O*nce we've deracinated these phlegmatic and
problematic dragons and ousted those two man-
hungry chatelaines, we'll move into the master
bedroom and north tower and try out that snazzy
salle de bain," said one of the captured bandits,
whose sleep-deprived delusions were dragging
them into a euphoria of soft pillows and oda-
lisques.[†]

dernier cri

the latest fashion, the last word

*O*h, it's the dernier cri!" yipped the usually unflappable *grande horizontale,* reaching for her escort's snuffbox, fan, and smelling salts as they entered the Schloss's *grand salon.*

epigone

a second-rate imitator or follower, especially of an artist or philosopher

*L*eft in the dust by Schlaffenfuss's prêt-à-partir hausfrau escape frocks was a flurry of haute couture epigones struggling with their suspenders and abandoned by their mannequins.

161

fainéant

literally, doing nothing: lazy

*T*he Schloss magnanimously welcomed volatile underdogs and fainéant parasites in addition to guests of great promise or virtuosity whenever they mounted its grand staircase or scuttled in by more clandestine passages.

farouche

fierce; sullenly unsociable or shy

*F*litting through the corridors like a frightened shadow was Katya's cousin Kristiana, a farouche fifteen-year-old whose topaz eyes lost that deranged look of theirs in the presence of the panther or little dragons.

fatidic

prophetic

Come to think of it, several weeks before the night that ended all his joy in life, King Alabastro had had a fatidic dream about Dariushka's demise, only she was disguised as a wildebeest being hunted down by a band of Boer pig farmers and was saved from such an ignoble finish by the jaws of an obliging tiger.

hegemony

the overriding influence or the dominance of one state over others

Blegue's hegemony over Lavukistan and Azuriko was a truncated affair indeed: it was more like a blind date in a parked car that was over before the sun had finished setting and the drive-in movie hit the screen.

imprimatur

sanction, approval—whether official or otherwise desired, sought

*T*hat production bears the unmistakable imprimatur of the Belladonna Mafia, so it's sure to pack in a crowd of goose-stepping nannies and some *hommes d'affaires* in drag," predicted Cedric Moltgang of the dramatization of *Giovanna's Mortgage* opening in Evrique.

Schlaffenfuss released his Ubiquitous Nightgowns on the Town without the imprimatur of his sometime patron Iztavo Stollenkranz, who'd backed his Wombat Fatigues in Isfahan, Inverness, and Eloria.

Imprimatur also means imprint.

The Loneliness of the Bluestockinged Mugger first appeared under the imprimatur of the Malcontessa Press, but after the first fulgurant print run, it was reissued—under an even more shocking cover—by the omnivorous Morrigan House.

inculpate

to incriminate, taint with blame

*B*y inculpating four of his buddies, Frotteau Dessange got off with an easy sentence: touching up the murals at the Ministry of Money and War and restoring the Wupertalers' Ballroom to its former fulminating frenzy.

internecine

mutually destructive or harmful; deadly or harmful to both sides of a group involved in a conflict

*O*h, bloody awful! Just what this group needs—an internecine squabble with microphones and biological weapons at hand," said Tyger Mischief as his supernumeraries surged out of control and hijacked his motion picture into a horror show.

The second decade of Troto's life as a soldier was devoted to an internecine war of such inscrutable savagery that the land for hundreds of miles was shrouded in a fulminating darkness for days on end, filled with cries of the wounded and bereft, haunted by the slaughtered.

inveigle

to entice or lure by artful talk, inducements, cajolery

*T*he troglodytes of Lavukistan were seized with an endemic of Tyrolomania and left the country in hordes—which, in their case, meant by the bubble-wrapped boxload or in trunks. Each one had to inveigle a former chum, cast-off cousin, or creaky grandmother into doing them up in natty packages and seeing them comfortably ensconced in some boxcar—with warnings to the outside world against sudden sociable gestures.

involute

rolled up or curled in a spiral

*T*hat"—Sigismund Lolotte Flint-Page gestured toward the involute form of silvery sheen on the damask ottoman—"is my greyhound puppy, Aldebrand, on a photocopy of *Gossamer and the Green Light,* my latest idée fixe."

lacuna

a gap, a space that's empty, a part that is
missing

I've called you here tonight on such short notice," began Amaranthia, addressing the assembled guests in their assorted deshabilles and
states of consciousness, "to fill in a few lacunae I
have noticed at the chapel and the breakfast
table . . . Some of you have gone missing or
slipped into shadows, are no longer visible to my
major-domo and me. Letters and telephone calls
encounter silence or an occasional muffled
scream like the ones that have been reported at
the national library of Blegue. The staff is on the
brink of insurrection, the dragons have left the
ground floor en masse, and outsiders are clam-
oring for tidings of those our five senses have
failed to locate with the best of intentions and
the worst of our fears."

There's that odd lacuna in the last chapter of *The
Bad-Tempered Cavalier:* the protagonist is just
about to hurl herself off the parapet when sud-
denly the page goes blank (did the author's
mind?), and next thing you know she's having her
heels sanded at Boris Marcelovsky's and exchanging betting tips with Nimbo Moostracht's
niece.

lambent

playing lightly upon or over a surface, flickering; easily light or brilliant; luminous, gently glowing

*D*ulac's lambent adumbration of the incipient dénouement sets the reader up for an exposé of the most trifling indiscretions and not the perfidious betrayals that actually unfurl at the end of her roman à clef *Tatiana's Bear.*

"I'm the mouse that's hard at play while the big bad cat's gone astray!" bellowed Beau Romano in response to a "Who goes there?" rattling through the darkness haunted by a lambent swirl of sulphurous light.

minatory

menacing, threatening

*M*ount Wafna is noted for not only its minatory mien and fatal angles, but also its history as the stamping ground of necromancers and fallen angels.

Count Ghastly opened the door with a minatory scowl, and once his guests were scattered about in congenial clusters of expectancy, the butler entered carrying a deck of cards and a stack of shrouds.

minion

a servile follower or subordinate of a person in power; a favored or highly regarded person; a minor official

*T*hose aren't holidaymakers and gamblers from the Casino of Bluttenbad. They're General Pvbxtrz's minions out for a night of whoring and mass arrests during an interlude of *Giovanna's Mortgage*.

Strophe Dulac usually gets one of her minions to pose for her publicity photos, since her readers all expect a less androgynous face staring back at them.

miscreant

a misbehaver, mischief-maker

*S*uspected miscreants were rounded up during the raid on the Pink Antlers Saloon (from the barstools, the branding iron, the pissing and powder rooms, the arcade of electronic horse-shoes and cattle-rustling games), conveyed by a convoy of lorries to the Seventh Spa, Inn of the Sixth Unhappiness, where they were finger-printed, deloused, and interrogated in broken English by officials from the diminished Lavuk-istan.

moribund

> near death or termination; in *very* serious
> decline! not progressing; stagnant, lifeless

*D*eclaring the Bosoxian pizza parlors a moribund proposition, Moostracht suggested they all be converted into columbaria and sold to Chichikov & Company.

"And now, a number for the moribundian contingent," announced the bandoneonist as he slowed his tango to a death march and the dandified cadavers swished onto the floor of Les Trottoirs de Buenos Aires in a languid rattle of bones, zippers, and false teeth.

moue

> a pout which might go so far as to seem a
> grimace (well, a little one)

*K*atya, catching a gleam of dagger in Drasko Mustafović's tone of voice, sauntered over to him on wounded knees and countered his next seven sentences with a moue of disarming grace.

nadir

lowest point

*H*istory may regard the Cashmere Crisis as the nadir of the entire Incognito succession, but the lapsed credenza hardly redounded to the credit of the family, either, even if it did end up at the Pink Antlers Saloon in a different story and century altogether, long after the king and his minions were last seen on the shores of Lake Quisisana.

narcoleptic

suffering from narcolepsy, a sickness of compulsive snoozing

*T*he little fellow is by no means narcoleptic," said the vet to Sonia as Pasha Partout swooned in her arms. "He's just a very excited somnambulist with too much sex appeal for his metabolism, plus a natural proclivity for plashing waters, cushions, thighs, generous bosoms, and Turkish delight in prodigal portions."

noetic

of or pertaining to the mind; originating in or apprehended by reason

*W*hat a noetic nougat!" said the novelist to his editor at Café Nada as they chattered their way from an ethereal apéritif to an imperceptible espresso.

non compos mentis

not of sound mind

*S*erafima Dos Equis was declared non compos mentis and sent off to the spa in Trajikistan where miraculous recoveries were being touted and where many government officials were malingering in the radioactive mud. But of course, this was just a ruse to place him in their midst to catch any indiscretions rolling off their lips as their edges blurred and they let down their carefully trained defenses.

non sequitur

> a reply or jump in conversation or writing that doesn't quite follow, make sense; an abrupt shift of logic or fix on a subject, or even a sabotage of logic

*H*owever, he found it difficult to sort out significant sound bites from the farrago of non sequiturs and aimless anecdotes in which these sycophantic cream puffs trafficked.

obloquy

> censure, blame, abusive language aimed at a person or thing by many or by the general public; discredit, disgrace, bad repute resulting from public blame, abuse, denunciation

*M*ay the obloquy of all the world rain upon your cracked and coronated cranium—and your children fall into this world with the Loud Hound of

Darkness snapping at their tails" was but one of the curses plaguing the reign of Prolix V (known fondly to his subjects as Prolix the Fey).

obviate

> to anticipate and prevent or eliminate (difficul-
> ties, disadvantages) by effective measures;
> render unnecessary: to *obviate* the risk of
> serious injury

*P*rolix IX obviated insurmountable objections to his ensuing edicts by hounding his ministers with impossible supplications from the mouths of implacable citizens and irresistible babes.

odalisque

> a female slave or concubine in a harem; an
> artistic representation of such a fantasy, all the
> rage among various painters enamored of
> fabric as well as flesh

*A*mong the aforementioned adorable babes was
an odalisque named Incredula Celsius, who pan-
tomimed her own wishes when the impulse
seized her and dragged her sorrows and bejew-
eled fingers through the weight of the others'
voices and their importunate behests.

palimpsest

> A **palimpsest**, which lends itself to metaphorical
> employment, is often used for works of classi-
> cal antiquity and refers to a manuscript written
> on vellum or parchment (or even papyrus) from
> which earlier text has been scraped before
> being written over—so partially effaced that the
> original text is still legible. This was before the
> days of delete buttons and backspace keys,
> when parchment was so valuable that it was put
> through multiple hands. The ghost of the old
> text often lingered beneath the new, leaving a
> double-exposure sense on the page.

*T*he map Jonquil held in her hands was perplexing indeed until her mentor explained that it was, in fact, an antique palimpsest, where outlines and details of the lost cities Viridu and Lamutatis were visible among the avenues and undulations of fin-de-siècle Blur.

"By God, I do believe what we have here is a palimpsest from several prolific generations of Lopalusians whose guilds dotted the flanks of Mount Oulipos in the seventeenth and eighteenth centuries," said the curator of the Mirudana Museum sotto voce to his assistant, Ipso Facto, whom he'd trained to suppress any signs of acquisitive urgency at estate sales, auctions, and bazaars.

paragon

> a model of excellence or perfection of a kind; a supreme example

*T*rill Apasaguena, the protagonist of *The Man in the Grey Flannel Suite,* evolved from a promising nonentity from Eloria into a paragon of pan-European cutthroat capitalism.

Ever a paragon among shooting stars, Mog wore her radiance with insouciance, her reputation with valor, her diadems with irony, her camisoles sans culottes.

parvenu

a person with newly acquired wealth, influence, acclaim—minus the social standing, acceptance to go with it: not yet attained

*H*e was a parvenu utterly without panache but was also a dead ringer for Serafima Dos Equis, which gave him an edge over beefier contenders for the mission of bombing the Ministry of Sports and Leisure.

Frodo Asgard, turning his attention to the audience and not the performance of *Desperadoes in Lace,* described patron Trill Apasaguena as "a parvenu who's just emerged from a greasy shadow, not a Fabergé egg."

pasquinade

a lampoon posted on a public place

$\mathcal{T}$his is clearly not the work of a sleepwalker shuffling through town at three a.m. or the afterthought of a drunken desperado, Sire," said Capriccio, delivering his report of the latest defamation: a pasquinade depicting Incognito VIII knitting booties of the finest cashmere in his corrugated pantaloons.

patois

> a regional form of a language, deviating from the usual one; figuratively: jargon, cant, argot

$\mathcal{T}$he patois around here is a curious, cacophonous blend of Romany and Donutrian, Oublanskaien, Samotrian dialects with handfuls of terms for courtship, brawls, and diplomacy bundled in from Bosoxia and Blegue.

profligate

> utterly, shamelessly dissipated, immoral; prodigal, recklessly extravagant

$\mathcal{P}$erhaps the greatest disgrace to the family was the king known as Prolix the Profligate, who certainly didn't live up to the first part of that name, since he had very little to say when asked where all the money had gone—which didn't matter, as the answer was obvious: he'd been flaunting his debaucheries and self-indulgence since he bought his first sapphire toothpick at the age of six and held slumber parties that went on for weeks. By the time of his death (face-first in a bidet filled with champagne), he had so thoroughly impoverished the royal coffers that his next two successors to the throne were both known as Prolix the Pauper and grew up innocent of the lure of gambling, expensive women, elegance in attire and notepaper, and had to rent out various wings of the royal palace as artisans' workshops, flower stalls, taverns, barracks, and bordellos.

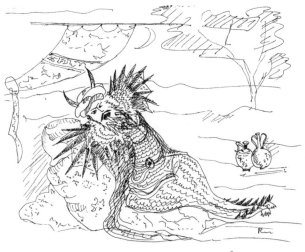

pythonic

of extraordinary size and power

"W here *shall* we put Pasha Partout once he attains his ultimate pythonic dimensions?" beseeched Sonia at the slightest scintilla of sympathy in the eye of a weekend guest.

quidnunc

a person all aflutter for news and gossip, a busybody (literally, "what now")

"O h—and tell that quadruped quidnunc to buzz off!" said Loona to the maître d'hôtel, waving toward a paparazzo posing as a waiter with miniature cameras in his cuff links and in the cameo of Queen Maud jerking about at his throat.

Well, I was quidnunc to the Court of Incognito VIII both before and after the Cashmere Crisis, so I could come up with a few names not yet implicated in that dossier you assembled through violence and venal arrangements.

redoubtable

evoking fear; fearsome; formidable; commanding respect or reverence

*M*ost redoubtable of all the brigands was Serafima Dos Equis, who was indeed a double-crossing angel with his honeyed phraseology, Botticellian fluidity and luminosity, clip-on wings for emergency exits, and duplicitous designs on half the traffic between Blegue and Azuriko.

What a redoubtable spot is the summit of Mount Wafna, with all the suspicious spirits that have cavorted there through the centuries.

refractory

obstinately resistant to authority or control

I can't decide which one is the most refractory," said Jacaranda as she and Amaranthia discussed the rampages of the little dragons and watched the cellist out of the corners of their eyes: it was certainly a face they'd seen at the Schloss, but did it belong to the owner?

retroussé

turned up, tucked up

nez retroussé

turned-up nose, snub nose

With her retroussé nose, her uplifted buttocks and eyebrows, her tautened chin, and silicone lips, Bambi returned from the Face Up Clinic with most of her physiognomy in a state of startled suspense.

riven

rent or split apart

All we have to go by is this riven piece of parchment that may be a map or a musical composition or a spell for repelling night visitors.

At the edge of the ravine stood a riven oak, the victim of a streak of lightning.

rubicund

red or reddish; ruddy

*O*h, Baby, rubicund will be all the rage this autumn with the advent of Signe Himmelstadt and her Bleeding Besonders Band!" exclaimed Boris Marcelovsky to a fishwife blonde resisting his bottles of Blushing Siena, Sanguine, and Transylvanian Twilight and asking for a simple shave and suntan, which came with a pedicure on the house or a pint of Smuggler's Stout.

sang-froid

literally coolness of blood, but used for coolness of mind, composure, unflappability

*F*amous for both her sang-froid and her quicksilver tongue, Mog could dance any death or disaster to that cliché of clicking needles: cool, calm, and collected.

scintilla

a touch, trace, iota: a minute amount; a spark or flash

I discerned barely a scintilla of interest in that look you gave me, and hardly a flicker of recognition, either," said Rip, reproaching an old flame who'd sauntered into the saloon as if ten years had flown by in the blinking of an eyelash.

Even when it's resting, the Loud Hound of Darkness emits scintillas of secret intelligence masquerading as manifestations of lightning.

seditious

> inciting discontent, rebellion against a
> government

*T*he country is roving with seditious women in pants and cowboys in flashy underwear who have nothing whatsoever against the government of Gavril Dark, but have printed up pamphlets of an inflammatory nature for the sake of a literary adventure.

sempiternal

> a literary, rather than street-corner, word for
> everlasting, eternal

*T*he House of Amaranth is indulging in a bit of wishful thinking, naming itself for an imaginary sempiternal flower.

"Is this bargain sempiternal, or shall we call it quits once I've lined up a couple of extraterrestrial gigolos?" asked the baba of her adversary, at the end of a sound thrashing in which neither had gained the upper hand, but which both had found most bracing.

"You're my sempiternal sidekick, my river of re-nunciation, my memento mori in the house of love," went one line of "This Train Stops Forever," composed by a laptop cowboy hanging out at the Pink Antlers.

somnolent

> sleepy, drowsy; producing this state, putting to sleep

*L*isten here, my little spitfire, I think it's time you lighten up and put those flashing fangs away," said Kristiana, who'd been sent out into the forest to placate the beast that had been hounding wayfarers from the east. She lowered her voice to a susurrant growl and fixed him with her most somnolent gaze, and soon the dreaded creature was licking her knees and stretching its draggled form at her feet.

"What a somnolent stupor is overcoming my vicious thunderclaps!" exclaimed Dariushka to the alchemist, who had given her a draught of his own devising to bring her excitation down to a level befitting a sovereign and expectant mother.

stridulous

A **stridulous** sound is harsh or grating, such as
a banshee might make while having a bit of fun
with some sandpaper and the full range of its
vocal cords.

*W*hat's that stridulous brouhaha that seems to be
coming simultaneously from the shut-off television and the attic?" Laurinda asked her husband
the first time Loona's wedding gift was announc-
ing its presence to them.

The audience set up a stridulous protest to the
kitschiness of the backdrop and libretto.

The night wore on endlessly and sleeplessly with
the rumble of distant cannon and unidentified
stridulous disharmonies that sounded like har-
pies in heat screeching while they banged on
tambourines from hell.

sui generis

unique; of his, her, its, their own kind

*N*ow's your chance to meet a *real* cowboy," said Yolanta to Laurinda, indicating a curious individual indeed with crossed legs and a shopworn shirt seated at the end of the bar. "Well, he is a cowboy sui generis, I admit," she went on, as she caught his eye and he waved a gloved hand in their direction, then returned to the lyrics on his laptop for "We Had a Continental Breakfast Kind of Love" and thought fondly, yet painfully, of his pal Rip, who had such a way with napkin rings and late late morning baths.

"Oh, I assure you this little roadster is a hellcat on the open highway, and this steering wheel is strictly sui generis—you won't find another like it in all of Laponesia," the Rara Avis agent was hyperbolizing to Trill Apasaguena, who was on a quest for a tailor all his own and had decided on a rented car to allow for improvisations and a bit of impulse shopping for subarctic curios.

sylvan

of the woods or forest; inhabiting them

*T*he faun, uprooted from his Mediterranean habitat and out of sorts in the shambles of Bluttenbad, took to spending afternoons by himself with thoughts of Effie the nymph and her sylvan, silvery laughter as she flitted through the slanting shade.

threnody

a song of lamentation, a dirge for the dead

The rats convened in a sylvan setting of Louvelandia to set up a full-throated threnody and consecrate to the earth and Eternity their many friends, relatives, and playmates the plague had carried off with its deadly emissaries, the fleas.

traduce

to speak maliciously and falsely of; to slander, defame; to slam with animadversions

I've been banished, I've been traduced, I've been booted out to seek my fortune in strange and difficult lands," wrote Jonquil in a small frantic notice for the *Amplochacha Asphodel,* a weekly alternative rag, along with a mug shot in which she might not be recognized by superficial acquaintances.

trumpery

> showy but worthless finery; frippery, bric-a-brac;
> something of no use or value: rubbish, trash;
> nonsense, twaddle

*T*hese allegations are sheer trumpery, and I'll call
out the hounds *and* my lawyers if you dare re-
produce them for frenzied public combustion.

13 ix   Immergau

Dear Amaranthia,

Can't say I hope all's well at the Schloss: I gave up,
as I know you did, on such vain enterprises long
ago. My weekend was foreshortened by a sudden
call to the bedside of my uncle, who, just between
the two of us (you and me, that is), I think is faking it so we'll pack him off to Trajikistan again.
Can't figure out if it's the place or someone he met
there that's got such a hold on him, but I'm looking for clues in his pockets while he sleeps off
the potion I slipped into his Calvados. Anyway,
tomorrow I must go over and tend to some of
his unfinished correspondence at the Immergau
Museum: tactful rejections of trumpery, trinkets,
contents of closets in crumbling châteaux, dis-
putable paintings (merely awful or else a question
of attribution), pleasure domes of playboys and
fetishes of entrepreneurs, not to mention the be-
quests of that aristocratic pack rat who's lighten-

ing up to humor her beau. Well, you get the picture; now I must return to my intimate investiga-
tions. See you soon should my wish be granted.

Your dubious major-domo,
Jacaranda

twee

too terribly precious or nice

*A*maranthia and Jacaranda tucked into a twee
boulangerie behind the mittelplatz of Lumbachen
for a Baroque serenade and feverish discussion
of the crisis at the Schloss following Drasko
Mustafović's abduction. Several infusions of
chocolate led them to two possible conclusions:
he was playing the cello in that very room—or he
was faking it (either the abduction or the cellist
impersonation: they were of several minds on
this point).

"We Twee Kings of Glorious Karst" was the
unofficial pop tune of the Trajikistani court—
with many bawdy, unprintable variants.

Nada Seria was hailed as the diva of twee upon the publication of her fifth romance novelette, *The Temptation of Tristan le Fay.*

unflappable

> not easily upset or confused, especially in a crisis; possessed of a resilient steadiness

*P*ulling up alongside the *Scarlatina* was a *bâteau louche* under a captain who'd been captivated by the sea of stories about the unflappable Ziggie Spurthrast.

"I've had it! This bordello calls for an unflappability with which I have not been blessed," said Amaranthia, blowing her stack so she could catch the last train to Amplochacha and the predatory prowl she'd promised herself for enduring a week of travail.

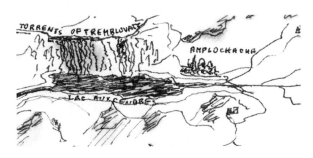

ungulate

having hoofs, or hooves

*S*lim, pert, frisky heifer seeks rough-mannered but gentle-natured ungulate male for forest floorings, botanical ambles, fireside spats.

uxorious

excessively devoted to, besotted with, submissive to one's wife, or, in this case, which takes liberties, one's intended, wished-for bride hallucinated into a wife

*A*stride a brisk young palomino was the uxorious inamorato of Dusty Saxon, his heart a darkened mass of the most grievous jealousy, his pantaloons flapping with nonchalance in the dawn's pearly luminescence.

viatic

of or related to travel, journeys, or else of a road, a way

*H*ave you any viatic counsel for me, before I take my leave? I can't figure out the swiftest or safest path to Le Lac aux Cendres, or which one to choose should these be revealed.

"But please, I must desist from these viatic vignettes of Oostricht, Ratizmir, and Bluttenbad, and my year among the last living Lopalusians, and beg you to shimmer me with some more legends of your phantasmagoric land," said Jonquil to the heirs apparent of Trajikistan's triple monarchy as she lit their cigarettes and fixed them with an implacable, inveigling chagrin.*

vitiate

> to mar, sully, or impair the quality of; to debase, corrupt, pervert

*I*t will only vitiate your afterlife if you continue to resist me," said the Grim Reaper to the baba as she dealt out a seventh hand of poker and wore with amazing grace the haunted look of a sure-fire winner.

* the only kind of smile permitted in the presence of the Trajikistani royal family

"The presence of Kristiana is vitiating the performance of the panther as the defender of our castle," wrote Amaranthia in a memo to the au pair who'd introduced her sister to the big bad cat of Mesmer eyes and breathtaking, sexy haunches.

volte-face

> an about-face, whether physical or figurative, as in a reversal of policy

*N*imbo Moostracht contemplated the humiliation of a volte-face, then decided instead on the devaluation of the zlotky, which would merely crush the hopes of a country already bankrupt from years of banditry, harlotry, and government-sponsored atrocities.

Sensing a head-on clash with a bewitched and bereaved battalion, General Ludović ordered an abrupt volte-face and took to his heels, weaving a spellbinding path to his accustomed table at Café Sans Souci.

zaftig

buxom, full-bosomed; having a pleasantly
plump figure, a voluptuous, shapely body

*W*ell, darling, too many afternoons of this cham-
ber music *mit gâteaux de chocolat* and we'll
turn into a couple of zaftig Sacher tortes our-
selves," said Jacaranda, seeking to spare herself
and Amaranthia further hallucinations starring
Drasko Mustafović in disguise or drag.

*C*ontrary to the most monstrous expectations of
everyone who'd ever inhabited or visited the
Schloss, Pasha Partout did not grow into a fainéant, enervated, zaftig lap dragon but a sentry,
warrior, and lover of stupendous stamina, furi-
ous momentum, impetuous pace, and stealthy
suppleness.

Index

About the Author

Karen Elizabeth Gordon is the author
of *The Deluxe Transitive Vampire,*
The New Well-Tempered Sentence,
The Red Shoes and Other
Tattered Tales, Paris Out of Hand,
The Disheveled Dictionary, and
Torn Wings and Faux Pas. She lives
in Berkeley, California, and France.

Drago Rastislav Mrazovac, who
created the drawings, is a Yugoslav
architect, urban planner, and artist
who lives in Paris.